AF809053

Your Retirement Lifeboats

How to Ensure Safe Passage Throughout Your Retirement

Mark J. Andra

Your Retirement Lifeboats

How to Ensure Safe Passage Throughout Your Retirement

Copyright © 2020 Mark J. Andra
All rights reserved.

Disclaimer

This publication is designed to provide accurate and authoritative information regarding the subject matter contained within. It should be understood that the author and publisher are not engaged in rendering legal, accounting or other financial service through this medium. The author and publisher shall not be liable for your misuse of this material and shall have neither liability nor responsibility to anyone with respect to any loss or damage caused, or alleged to be caused, directly or indirectly by the information contained in this book. The author and/or publisher do not guarantee that anyone following these strategies, suggestions, tips, ideas or techniques will become successful. If legal advice or other expert assistance is required, the services of a competent professional should be sought.

All rights reserved. No portion of this book may be reproduced mechanically, electronically, or by any other means, including photocopying, without written permission of the author. It is illegal to copy the book, post it to a website, or distribute it by any other means without permission from the author

Expert Press

www.ExpertPress.net

Table of Contents

Note to the reader: I began writing this book over the mild summer months of 2019, when we were experiencing one of the greatest economic booms in U.S. history. As I near the completion of it in April 2020—during the worldwide COVID-19 pandemic—it is clear to me that most of what you're about to read in this book, regarding a safe and comfortable retirement, has proven applicable and even prophetic!

That's not to say I'm a prophet. The facts within this book proved true because they're **always** true. Whether you are reading this in the midst of the economic distress caused by COVID-19 or enjoying the calmer waters of a post-pandemic boom, the lessons in this book will be applicable.

Please read carefully and take care of your physical and financial health.

INTRODUCTION

If you were somehow transported back to 1912 and placed on the deck of the Titanic right before it set sail, what would be your first concern? Assuming you couldn't get off immediately, you'd most likely find out where the lifeboats were and spend all your time near them.

Unlike all the other passengers, you would know that this ship—claimed at the time to be indestructible—would meet its end in the North Atlantic in just a few days. Despite the exuberance of the passengers and the certainty of Captain Edward Smith, you would know why the Titanic would go down in history.

But what if I told you that today, in 2020, you are already a passenger on the deck of another Titanic? What if I told you that this ship, just like its predecessor, is certain to crash in the not-too-distant future? What would you do then?

I hope you'd do the very same thing: run to the lifeboats and get ready to launch to safety in the sea.

From Noteworthy to Tragic

The Titanic is the most famous ship in history for all the wrong reasons. On its maiden voyage, it was filled with wealthy celebrities—and far more individuals of modest means. Then on April

14, 1912, at 11:40 p.m., the ship hit an iceberg, and 2 hours and 40 minutes later sank into the Atlantic.

Of course, the fact the ship that some claimed to be unsinkable actually sank would have always made the moment noteworthy in history, but that isn't what made the moment a tragedy. The tragedy of the Titanic was the number of lifeboats.

So confident was Captain Smith in his ship, he didn't bother to ensure there were enough lifeboats to carry all the passengers to safety in the event he had miscalculated the strength of his vessel. Because of this oversight, when the Titanic hit that iceberg, the risk was not just to the ship but to the approximate 2,208 passengers on board. In the end, only 705 survived.

The crew and passengers were so poorly prepared for a crash that even those lifeboats that were on board were misused and underutilized. In theory, there was enough space to carry 1,178 passengers—about half—off the ship. Instead, most of those lifeboats were launched half full. In the most extreme case, a 45-person boat held only 12 occupants, two of which were dogs.

We're All on Board the Titanic Today

It's a tragic story, but what does that have to do with you? Like I said at the beginning, you may think you're living a life on solid ground, but in fact, you're on the Titanic right now. We're living in an economy destined for a crash, and if you are retired or about to retire, you're in the worst possible position to survive it. So, the lessons you take from that long-sunken ship could save you and your retirement.

In particular, there are two lessons I hope you keep in mind. First, never assume that anything is indestructible, no matter what others tell you. Everything sinks, breaks, or crashes eventually. And second, prepare for that inevitability by making sure you have enough lifeboats.

The Unsinkable Economy

Of the 705 who survived the Titanic, the vast majority were the elite, super-wealthy passengers on board. They had the best cabins with easy access to the lifeboats once events turned toward the worst. Most of those who didn't survive were the middle-class passengers below deck, the ones who worked hard and saved for their trip, but who couldn't afford a place that would have ensured their survival.

Unfortunately, we are seeing these same dynamics play out in our economy today. In many ways, we could easily call this a "Titanic economy." The stock market is extremely robust—which lifts all of us, but the wealthy more than the rest. That would be fine, but the market is also extremely overvalued. It is due for a correction at any time, and when that correction hits, it will be thunderous. Who do you think is in a position to escape that crash without harm? And who is going down with the ship?

The answer to that second question, unfortunately, is probably: you.

I can say that with confidence because we've been through this before. In the last 20 years, we've seen two major corrections. In each case, the losses were substantial, and the ones to suffer the most were the middle-class retirees with their savings invested in the stock market they had been told would just keep rising.

We are steering directly for the next correction right now, and those of you who depend upon retirement savings invested in the market are just like those middle-class passengers on the Titanic. You've managed to save your way into the price of the ticket, but you aren't positioned well enough to ensure a seat on one of the lifeboats.

Your only options are to sink or get your own lifeboats.

Your Broker: Captain Smith

Of course, if you bring this up to your broker, they'll dismiss your concerns. "Yes," they will tell you, "the market will hit a correction; it always does. And then it always bounces back."

Just like Captain Smith, they'll tell you not to worry. "This market is indestructible," they'll say.

And they'll be right. Given a long enough timescale, the market is indestructible. After the last two corrections, the market regained its full value over time. Within a few years, it was back where it had been, and then it started to grow again.

So the market does always bounce back … but that doesn't mean everybody bounces back with it. The problem is not everyone can wait for the bounce. Especially vulnerable are those drawing income from their accounts during the bounce. The double whammy of market losses coupled with systematic withdrawals sank many retirement boats during past corrections. In fact, during both recent corrections, millions of retirement accounts were wiped out, and the retirees who owned them were left to struggle for the rest of their retirement.

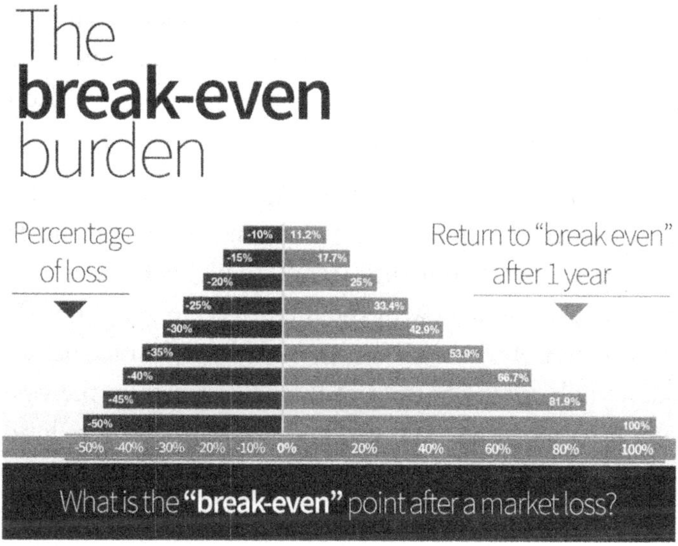

What your broker means, then, is that the market is indestructible *for some people*. Younger and wealthier investors regained everything. The others, like you perhaps, could get abandoned on the sinking ship.

Where You Are on the Boat Matters

The biggest mistake I see from those of retirement age is that they continue to pursue the same financial strategies that worked for them in their 20s, 30s, and 40s. By the time they reach their late 50s and beyond, their financial needs have changed, but they keep the same investment strategies, expecting the same outcomes.

When you were younger, you were in a position to take some financial risks. If you lost money in your 401(k), that was fine. You were still working, and you weren't using that money anyway. Your concern during a downturn was keeping your job, not maintaining a steady income out of a retirement account. Now, as retirement approaches, you need that money not for accumulation but to live on. And because of that, your days of risk and uncertainty are behind you. Those days have been replaced by a need for guarantees and safety.

A middle-class person remaining fully in the market during retirement is the equivalent of changing rooms on the Titanic. Over the course of your entire working life, you had a nice room on the deck with a view of the lifeboats. Now, right as the ship enters icy waters, you've been moved to a room far below deck. Today, you're at the bottom of the boat. You're in the worst position for a recession. And yet, that is just where we're heading.

Your 37 Seconds

On the Titanic, there were 37 seconds between the sighting of the iceberg and the actual crash. Had the ship carried enough lifeboats and had the crew been organized, those 37 seconds could have made all the difference in how many people survived.

Those on the Titanic wasted that opportunity, but the good news for you is, you also have those same metaphorical 37 seconds. You can see the iceberg ahead, and you can make the changes necessary by adding lifeboats to your financial ship. That way, you can sail off to a comfortable retirement, no matter what the market does.

So what are you going to do with your 37 seconds? You can sit tight and hope the economy misses the big iceberg ahead. Or you can hope the economy is so indestructible that any downturn is small enough it won't hurt your retirement plans.

But I'd like to suggest a third option: Start looking for and positioning yourself into a lifeboat now. We all like to assume that bad things don't happen to good people, but that isn't the case. Plenty of good people went down with the Titanic: hardworking people who did everything right and were just unlucky. Likewise, plenty of good people saw all their savings wiped out in the last two market corrections.

This has been one of the best economies in recent memory,[1] but it is still going to hit an iceberg, and plenty of good people are still going to get hurt by that. You don't have to be one of them, but to avoid that fate, you've got to take matters into your own hands.

The clock is ticking, the lookout on the bow is imploring you to take action now!

A Career Spent Looking for Lifeboats

I know about these risks because I've dedicated my entire career to helping people get into retirement lifeboats before it was too late. Since 1990, I've been an industry leader in giving retirement advice to those who find themselves in the mid-to-lower decks of retired America. Over that time, I've played a key role in helping more than 6,000 individuals and families secure the retirement they've earned through their hard work, sacrifice, and planning. I've become an expert in identifying safe and secure financial lifeboats, and I pride myself on my ability to pack anyone who's willing safely on board before the iceberg hits.

1 At least until the emergence of COVID-19 in early 2020.

I've built my career upon steering everyone who walks into my office toward the best strategies for them based on their unique financial situation, age, risk tolerance level, and needs.

And I don't believe in keeping this information private. I want everyone to know, because I want everyone to be able to retire with dignity and comfort. That's why I don't just wait for people to walk into my office; I also give 32 public seminars every year, educating all who want to hear about safe and guaranteed options for retirement income and planning.

And that's why I've written this book. Within these pages, I'll provide you with free resources and advice, so you can get started finding your way to the lifeboats that will keep you safe and secure in this current and future Titanic economies.

If You're in the Retirement Age Group, Listen Up

This book has advice that is useful for everyone, but it's critical for those of retirement age, from about 55 to 80. Now, within that age group there will be a small number of people who won't need this book. Those are the super-wealthy—the fortunate few—who are certain to escape the ship when it hits the iceberg. They've got plenty of resources and options, no matter what is ahead. So I'm not going to concern myself with their financial pictures—although I certainly welcome them taking what lessons they can from what follows.

Equally, if you're 34, you're not ready for this book. You're working and saving, and you'll ride out the next recession and probably the next one after that before you need to worry about the advice in this book. You've got time.

Instead, I've made this book for those of you who have limited resources and limited time. You may have Social Security, a decent-sized 401(k) or other retirement account, and perhaps a home. In total, though, your assets would add up to less than $2 million. Should the economy keep going as it is now forever, you could be able to get by, but you are in no position to weather rough waters. And if we hit another iceberg, you could be one of those stories of the left behind.

You aren't alone. According to the Transamerica Center for Retirement Studies, 96% of American families do not retire comfortably. Most of those people worked hard all their lives and saved all they could. And yet, at the end of their careers, they have a modest retirement account and perhaps a valuable house. This group could be described as the proverbial property rich and cash challenged.

This is particularly true for retirees living on the east and west coastal regions of our country. People there live in some of the most prosperous real estate markets on the planet, which are also some of the most expensive cost of living locations.

Retirement is always expensive, and unfortunately, it can become completely unaffordable if you see your sources of income hit by an iceberg.

But that doesn't mean you have to be at risk for sinking into those icy waters. Using only the assets you already have, we can construct lifeboats that will see you through any crash and keep you comfortable and afloat.

There are three powerful lifeboats available to most middle-class American families that could set you sailing smoothly throughout your golden years. And I'm about to show you how to maximize each of these vessels for a more comfortable and safe retirement.

Part I

Where I Learned About Lifeboats

Chapter 1.

My Dad Was My First Client

I didn't start out expecting to spend my career helping people survive the inevitable crashes in our Titanic economy. Instead, at first, I seemed destined for a far more traditional career as a financial advisor.

In 1986, I graduated from the Marriott School of Management with a Bachelor of Science degree in Business/Marketing. My first job following graduation was as an income property broker for a midsize investment real estate firm in San Francisco, where I worked with the wealthy landlords of the Bay Area on some of the most expensive real estate on the planet.

During the mid-to-late 1980s, approximately 58% of the people living in the Bay Area could not afford to buy a home (it's even less affordable now). Most who lived and worked near San Francisco had no other alternative but to rent. That obviously made for a very good investment for those who had the money to own residential income property.

My job was to bring wealthy buyers and sellers of residential income property together and to negotiate prices and terms that were agreeable to all parties. In 1986, I was the top-producing income property broker at my firm, and I had a bright career ahead of me in a very lucrative field. There was nothing stopping me from becoming a super-successful broker in the uber-competitive Bay Area investment real estate market, except one thing: I didn't feel fulfilled in my work. I wasn't really changing lives or helping people who really needed me. All I was doing was helping those who had plenty to have a little more. That purpose may be fine for some, but I wanted to do something that changed lives and gave my life's work a little more meaning and satisfaction.

The Moment It All Changed

Then, in 1990, as the president of my own income property brokerage firm in San Diego, an opportunity came my way. I was working with a client who had just sold a large shopping center and wanted to complete a tax-free exchange into some apartment units. My client was nearing retirement, and he felt apartments would pay out more consistently over time. However, in order to complete this transfer tax-free, I would have to identify three suitable exchange properties within 45 days.

This was obviously a very stressful time, but after many exhausting days, I approached my meeting with this investor client quite pleased with my findings. I had found just what he was looking for. Yet, when I introduced the fruits of my hard work to my client, he didn't sign on, he threw out the whole idea.

"Mark," he told me, "I hate to break your heart, but I'm not going to buy those apartments in San Diego, nice as they may be. In fact, I'm not buying apartments at all anymore."

"You've got to be kidding me," I said. "I've been looking all over heaven and earth, and now that I've found the perfect up-leg property, you're not going to invest in real estate anymore? What are you going to do with the taxable proceeds from the sale of your shopping center?"

He gave me an almost conspiratorial look. He was going to let me in on his big secret as a reward for all the effort I'd put in.

He said, "I've found a safe and secure way to produce a lifetime income that I prefer over tenants, termites, and toilets. They're often used for retirement planning, and since I'm about to enter retirement myself, they're simply too good to pass up.

"And listen," he added. "Since you've worked so hard and have been so loyal to me throughout this process, I'd be willing to buy these tax-deferred savings plans from you."

Of course, I had to admit that I had never heard of such a plan but promised that I would do my best to provide what he wanted. I bought a $300 manual that taught me about these "tax-deferred saving plans" and got a state license so I could legally offer them to my client. I then proceeded to help my client transfer his after-tax sale proceeds into these safe income-producing accounts—which we'll cover in more detail in Part III.

I thought that would be the end of it. In fact, I might have forgotten about the whole event if it wasn't for my dad. He was the one to show me that this wasn't a one-off situation with a now-former real estate client; this was my new career.

My First Customer

My dad has always been my number one supporter in everything I've ever done. When I started playing Pop Warner football in the summer of 1969, my dad became the team equipment manager and, eventually, club president three years later. During my high school and college football playing days, he attended every game. When I sold books during the summer months while in college, my dad bought books from me. When I started selling apartments in San Francisco following graduation, my dad saved up, scraped together some money from the sale of a home he'd bought in the early '60s, and bought a six-unit fixer-upper.

I was blessed to have one guaranteed customer, cheerleader, and supporter in life! So when I found out about this tax-deferred savings plan for retirees, I immediately thought of him.

In 1990, my dad was 59 years old, and retirement was on his mind. He intended to retire at 62 in just three years, but his finances weren't as strong as he might have liked. He had spent his career owning and operating a pool business in Beverly Hills, California. This had earned him enough to buy his home (only $39,500 at the time—imagine that!) and put my sisters and me through school.

He'd done fine in life, financially, but he wasn't sure how to keep doing fine once he retired. He'd seen too many Black Mondays to trust his retirement to a mutual fund. He'd experienced enough icebergs to know he couldn't be sure he'd survive another one without his pool business.

It seemed to me that I should talk to my dad about this new secure retirement account that I had just discovered. It might help him ease his way into retirement.

I called him up the next day and said, "Dad, I've got something to tell you about your retirement."

"Great," he said, "I've got something to tell you, too. But you go first."

"I was recently informed by one of my real estate clients about this savings account that's great for retirement income."

I told him all the details, and his response surprised me. He laughed.

"Mark," he told me, "I just went down to the bank the other day and bought that exact same plan."

"You've got to be kidding me!" I said, shocked.

"Not at all," he replied, "and since the paperwork isn't finalized at the bank yet, I'll buy them from you instead."

I suppose there must have been something in the air that day. Somehow, my dad and I discovered this tax-deferred savings plan at the same time, and we were both convinced of its merits immediately.

Specializing in Maximizing Limited Resources

Seeing how this new retirement account changed my dad's life convinced me that I had been in the wrong line of work. I'd felt more satisfaction helping Dad navigate retirement with his limited resources than in all the big deals I'd worked on in San Francisco and San Diego.

I realized that there must be thousands of people in the area just like Dad—people who were looking to secure their retirement but who might not know how to do it. Unlike all my previous clients in the Bay Area, they didn't have an accountant to call to answer their questions and discover the best investment strategies. They didn't have expensive financial advisors to make sure every dollar returned two, no matter the state of the economy. These people were navigating one of the most difficult transitions of their lives completely on their own.

And if I could help my dad navigate the uncertain waters of retirement, I could help other people like him as well.

I decided on that day to pursue a career as a Retirement Planning Specialist for those with limited resources—those who couldn't afford to mess things up. I was going to help that group plan and prepare for a more comfortable retirement, just like I did for Dad!

That's what I've been doing for the last 30 years. And now, I'm looking to help you do the same.

Chapter 2.

The Tip of the Iceberg

I told you the story in Chapter 1 because I want you to know that my interest and focus on retiring comfortably has been a career-long goal. I've been watching for and helping others avoid icebergs for three decades now, and I'm quite certain that one is ahead. I've helped thousands of clients retire successfully, so when I say we're heading for rough waters, I want you to know where my passion comes from when guiding you toward a safe and comfortable retirement.

I can already hear your objections.

"How bad could it be, really?"

"Everything looks pretty stable to me!"

"So what? If the market hits a small bump, it's strong enough to rally quickly without putting much of a dent in my retirement savings!"

That sort of thinking is far too common amongst retirees today, and that same thinking was pervasive before the launch of the Titanic. In April 1912, everyone knew it was the season for icebergs, and they knew the risk of launching without careful precautions. Yet, so certain was everybody that nothing could sink that ship, caution was thrown to the wind.

Today, everyone knows an adjustment is looming—you've almost certainly heard whispers of words like "recession" or "correction"—but we've convinced ourselves that things are going so well, nothing could really hurt us.

In both cases, the consensus was dangerously far off. And in both cases, some people met a terrible fate because they assumed bad things just couldn't happen to them.

Gross Domestic Product (GDP) Compared to the Wilshire Total Market Index

Ratio = Total Market Cap / GDP	Valuation
Ratio < 50%	Significantly Undervalued
50% < Ratio < 75%	Modestly Undervalued
75% < Ratio < 90%	Fair Valued
90% < Ratio < 115%	Modestly Overvalued
Ratio > 115%	Significantly Overvalued
Where are we today **(05/28/2020)**?	Ratio = **142.8%** **Significantly Overvalued**

The Most Overvalued Market in History

Warren Buffett, one of the most successful investors alive, has developed a formula to determine when the market is set for an adjustment. He's developed this formula so he and his associates at Berkshire Hathaway know when the climate is right to invest heavily and when to be more careful.

To create this formula, Buffett looked at market performance over the past several decades. He was looking for an easy, foolproof way to calculate how the market was doing. There's a lot of noise in investing, and he wanted a quick way to take the temperature of the economy. And he found it. Buffett discovered that if you compared the total value of stocks to GDP (gross domestic product), you could get a good idea of when the market was headed toward a correction. According to Buffett, when the Wilshire Total Market index soars to 115% or more of GDP, we enter iceberg territory.[2]

Total Market Cap and US GDP

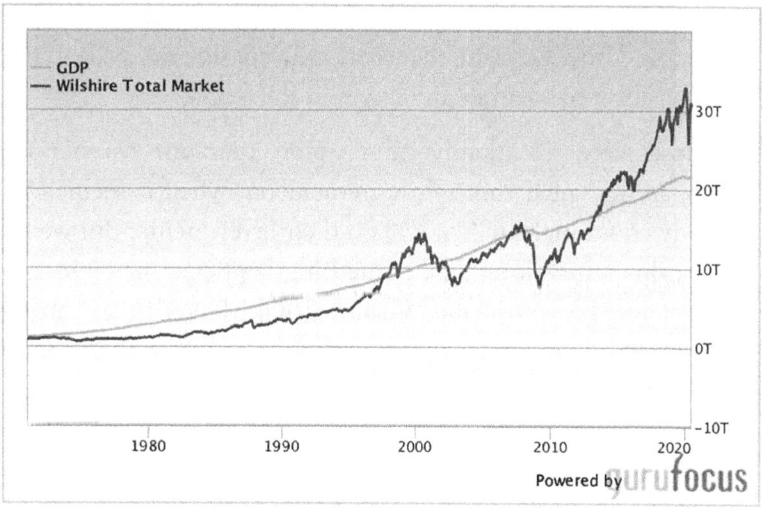

As you can see from the chart above, the Wilshire Total Market index from 1970 to 1998 kept within the 70% to 80% of GDP.

Buffett found that the historical average of the value of all stocks in relation to the GDP was about 74%. So long as the Wilshire Total Market index stayed within 75% to 90% of GDP,

2 We actually hit that iceberg in March 2020. However, there's much reason to hope for a full recovery soon. Even in those circumstances, though, we'll still be due for ANOTHER correction before long.

this would indicate a fairly valued market and a good time to buy. But when the value of all stocks sail beyond GDP—at about 115%—the market is deemed overvalued and an adjustment is just over the next crest.

We've Seen This Iceberg Before

As you can see from that graph, the Wilshire Total Market index from 1970 to 1998 kept within 70% to 80% of GDP. Of course, there were mini peaks and valleys, as there always are, but the market was relatively stable and growing. If we were living in that economy, you would be entirely right to dismiss my warnings in this book. You'd be right that, generally speaking, you'd be in a good position to weather any waves in the market.

Those were remarkably calm waters that our parents and grandparents sailed through retirement on, when it seemed everybody could make 6% or 7% on their investments. But we left those calm waters long ago. Something happened in 1998, and the roof was blown off the Wilshire Total Market index. Stocks began to climb at a massive rate, hitting a record peak in March 2000. The cause was the Roaring '90s of the Clinton administration when technology and the internet first supercharged our economy. The result in March 2000 was an unheard of (at the time) stocks to GDP ratio of 148.5%.

And what happened after that? Just as Buffett's model predicts, 34 months later, the Wilshire Total Market index went from 148.5% of GDP to 77%. Some people in the market lost 47% of their portfolio value. That was a whole lot of retirement accounts wiped out because no one prepared their lifeboats, even when the iceberg was in sight.

Buffett Predicts 50% Losses

So, how does our current market stack up in Buffett's calculation? Look back at that GuruFocus graph on page 27, and you can see it's one of the most overvalued in history. As of January 30, 2020, the Wilshire Total Market index was 151.1% of GDP, exceeding the previous record of 148.5% in March 2000. Buffett warned shareholders in a recent letter that losses of 50% or more were not only probable, they were inevitable![3]

That's right. One of the smartest investors on the planet has predicted that we are about to see 50% of the wealth in the market disappear, and a big part of that 50% is middle-class retirement savings.

So, ask yourself, are you comfortable enough today that you could survive retirement on only half of what you've saved? If the answer is no, it's time to head for the lifeboats.

3 This letter was published long before the world was introduced to the COVID-19 pandemic in December 2019 and was not even figured into his calculus at the time!

Chapter 3.

No Margin for Error

Some people lost 47% of their retirement savings in December 2002 when the market became unsustainably overvalued. Today, people are likely to lose even more. For some, losing even 47% of their savings wouldn't actually matter much to their daily lives. After all, if Warren Buffett lost 50% of his $80 billion fortune, he'd still have $40 billion left over. You might wonder whether he'd even miss a night of sleep since his modest home in Omaha, Nebraska, has been paid off since 1959!

For the 4% of the retired population who are super-wealthy, market fluctuations are more about inconvenience. They may not be able to purchase that second yacht or that fourth mansion until their investments recover a bit.

For the rest of us, though, we can't afford to be so cavalier, because for us, a correction quickly becomes a matter of survival. Imagine waking up one morning to find out your salary had been cut in half. How would you make it through the month, let alone the next couple of decades?

That's the kind of existential threat the market is posing to some middle-class Americans' retirement accounts right now.

Remember, when the Titanic went down, the rich were able to get into the lifeboats. It was the middle class who were left behind to deal with the tragedy.

What a Loss Looks Like for You

But are you really in such bad shape? After all, you saved over the whole course of your working life, and the money in your retirement account may seem inexhaustible at this point. Surely, even in the event of a significant market crash, you'd be able to recover.

Well, let's test that theory. Let's run your savings account through the first part of this century to see what your account would look like after the market became overvalued.

If we turn the clock back to the year 2000, we can see with 20/20 clarity what happened to even a relatively large retirement account. Let's say on January 1, 2000, you had $1,000,000 in an unprotected IRA tied to the performance of the S&P 500 index. At that time, the S&P 500 index was at 1,570. Two years later, we know that the market would hit a correction period. At that point, the S&P 500 index dropped by 50%, down to an index value of 800, which would mean your IRA would be valued at $500,000.

With a value of only $500,000 in your IRA, you'd probably do the natural thing and call your broker. Your broker, like Captain Smith before them, might tell you not to worry.

"Markets always suffer corrections," they'd say. "And they always come roaring back."

They'd then tell you that what you see in your statement just amounts to a "paper loss" and not to worry. The market would be growing again soon!

"Sit tight. Hold on," they'd say.

They'd say all this with supreme confidence, and they'd be confident because they'd be right. The market does always recover ... eventually.

After 2002, the market regained all its value by 2005. If you'd kept all your money in up to that point, you'd be back to where you started from and have $1,000,000 in your IRA again. Of course, in 2009, we know that the index fell by 60%, taking your account value down to $400,000.

Again, you might call your broker, and again they'd tell you the same story and not to worry about these "paper losses."

So, you might hold on for another few years and, lo and behold, by 2013 you'd have your $1,000,000 back after the S&P 500 did roar back by 120%.

It turns out, your stockbroker was right, and if you were still young through those downturns, there wouldn't be much to argue with them about. Here's the thing, though, you aren't young anymore. You can no longer afford to "sit tight" and wait for the market to correct itself. If you were taking income during the period of 2000 to 2013—instead of "sitting tight"—you'd be well on your way to running out of money!

Because you're retired, these are no longer "paper losses." The money in your account is real because it's what you have to live on. All of a sudden, those are real losses, and when the next downturn comes, you are going to be feeling real pain.

No Longer "Paper Losses"

When you are still working, what happens to your IRA is somewhat hypothetical. It's all just numbers on a piece of paper, as your broker tells you. But once you're taking money out of that IRA to live on, losses become very real.

If you were receiving 5% on the $1,000,000 in your unprotected IRA in 2000, you were living on $50,000 a year. That, plus your Social Security, may have left you living in reasonable comfort. But by 2002, you were making 5% on $500,000. While Buffett may not notice the difference between $80 billion and $40 billion, you would certainly notice the difference between $50,000 a year and $25,000 a year.

It would have been even worse in 2009, when your 5% on your $400,000 would have left you with just $20,000 a year to live on.

In the first case, you were comfortable. In the second case, you were struggling. In the third case, you may have been destitute.

And the news gets even worse. Because you're taking money out of your IRA, there's less money in your account to recover over time. When the market doubled in value between 2002 and 2005, your account could have returned to $1,000,000 in value—but only if you didn't touch it. Taking out 5% a year, there was far less within the account to double. If you took out $200,000 before the market hit those new highs, you could have only hit $600,000 before the next crash. After that crash, you would have been down to $240,000. It's much harder to recover that missing million in your savings from that position.

While the market may recover each time, you are no longer in a position to see all that money recover in your account. If you don't act wisely, you may end up living on less for the rest of your retirement.

These Are Your Playoffs

Your reaction to that may be, "That's not fair!" And I agree with you. It isn't. But as I said in the introduction to this book, you have to remember that bad things can happen to good people. Plenty of people who did everything right went down with the Titanic. Plenty of people who did a lot wrong got off the boat, just because they had the wealth to buy a better room closer to the lifeboats.

In retirement, it is sometimes the case that you can do everything right in your career and in your savings and still end up losing.

Middle-class retirement is like the NFL playoffs. You could play the perfect regular season, score more touchdowns than any team in history, and shut out every team you play. Still, once you're in the playoffs, all it takes is one mistake. It could be an interception or a fumble. It could be an injury to a crucial player. It may have nothing to do with you at all.

But with that one mistake, you can lose the game. And when you lose a playoff game in the NFL, you go home! It doesn't matter what records you set beforehand.

That can feel unjust. Just ask Tom Brady how he feels about the season the Patriots had a record of 18-0 heading into the Super Bowl. I doubt he remembers it fondly. Because they lost in the Super Bowl that year, all they did before was wiped out by that one loss.

This is why it is not prudent for a middle-class, retired American to gamble 100% of their retirement assets in the market during the distribution phase of their golden years. More caution should be taken. You're in the NFL playoffs now, and you can't afford even the smallest of errors at this point. One miscalculation, one unforeseen correction,[4] and you're sent home with a loss that you may never recover from. You have to do everything possible to get the win right now, because this is the win that matters.

This is how it works for middle-class America. One mistake—one blip in the economy—and your hopes of a long, comfortable retirement are over.

This is not the World Series where you have seven chances. Only the super-wealthy get those kinds of odds. You've got to make sure your money is right where it needs to be today, in foolproof retirement accounts that ensure you can't lose the one game that really matters.

And because the numbers indicate that this market is heading toward a correction, time is of the essence here. It may not look like it today, but you're riding a 1-point lead and the other team is inching closer to the end zone. You've only got a few plays left. You better make them count.

Time and Money Make All the Difference

You have no margin of error in this moment for two reasons. First, you've run out of time to make mistakes. If you were 32, you would have lots of time to wait for the market to correct and start growing again. You'd still be in the "paper losses" days when a downturn just looked like smaller figures on your IRA statements.

Likewise, if you had more money, you could insulate yourself against major losses. You would probably have far more sources of income and could weather almost any loss on the market.

4 Like COVID-19 in 2020.

But if you are like 96% of Americans and you don't have those huge resources, and if you're at or approaching the age of retirement, there's no more room to maneuver out of this situation. The ship is going to strike an iceberg. There's no time to correct course. And you aren't going to swim for it.

Some brokers won't tell you any of this because they are like Captain Smith: They're so confident in the market, and they can't see what the iceberg is going to do to their client.

If you're between 55 and 75, and you have modest assets—somewhere between $100,000 and $2,000,000 or so, including your home—you're going to have to find a lifeboat to take you to safety.

It's sink or swim time, and I don't want you to sink. So, we've got to find those lifeboats.

Chapter 4.

You Don't Have to Go Down With the Ship

So far, I've painted a somewhat dire picture here. We're careening toward an unhappy meeting with an iceberg, and you're in the worst possible position on the ship.

The market may be good today, but we know from history and the best analysis out there that it won't remain this good for much longer. That adjustment is just around the corner.

No one knows exactly when or how bad that correction will be, but we can predict who the losers will be: middle-class retirees.

It is mid-April, we are in the middle of the Atlantic, and this ship is heading straight for dangerous waters.

The Way to the Lifeboats

Now here's the good news. I know the way to the lifeboats. I've helped my dad onto them, and I've helped 6,000 other people onto them, as well. I'm a lifeboat expert, and I specialize in getting people like you—people with modest assets and a long, happy retirement ahead of them—onto the lifeboats that can sail straight out to calmer, more secure waters.

In fact, there are three types of lifeboats that every middle-class American nearing retirement needs to know about and climb aboard:

- the most underutilized lifeboat
- the unused-but-available lifeboat
- the unsinkable lifeboat

You may not be in that top 4% of the ultra-wealthy, but with my guidance, you can still have plenty of options.

That doesn't mean the ride is going to be easy. These are complex options, and it's easy to get them wrong. In fact, many end up in treacherous waters simply because they misuse the lifeboats set out for them.

That's why we're going to cover each lifeboat in detail, one at a time, so that you know how to steer them and where to go with each one.

Part II

Your Most Underutilized Lifeboat

Chapter 5.

Social Security Is a Complex, Important Stream of Income

I've been providing my dad with retirement advice for more than 30 years, and because of that, he's been able to live comfortably throughout his retirement. But because I wasn't an expert in all aspects of retirement planning when my dad actually retired, he made one mistake, and that mistake continues to haunt us both.

In 1993, my father was turning 62 and wondering what to do about his Social Security benefits. At that point in my career, I didn't have much expertise in the area of Social Security maximization planning, so I was unable to help him make the right choices. His accountant and attorney also knew nothing about entitlement benefit planning, so my father had to take this part of his retirement journey alone. He had no reliable source to turn to with his Social Security questions.

At that time, before the internet took off, it was much harder to find financial advice, even on something as important as Social

Security. If no one in your immediate circle knew how to navigate the program, there were few options available other than to just guess and hope you got it right.

That's just what happened to Dad. None of the people he normally relied upon knew much about how Social Security worked, yet he was approaching the age when he would have to decide when to take his benefits. As his birthday approached, he had to make a decision: start his benefits now or keep working and wait a few years.

With these choices revolving in his mind, Dad found himself one day at Costco, his favorite place to shop. As he was walking by the meat department, he saw his good friend, Butcher Bob. They exchanged greetings, and then, Butcher Bob leaned across the window and said—without any knowledge of my dad's dilemma, "Mr. Andra, I have a hot tip for you today. And it's not about the tri-tip."

"Great," my dad said, "I'm in need of a few tips lately. What is it?"

"I've just heard that the Social Security fund is going broke. They don't want to let on because they don't want to cause a panic, but they're going to cut Social Security soon. If you're eligible, I recommend that you take your Social Security benefits now."

My dad thought it was weird to hear inside information on government solvency at Costco, but Bob was a USDA-approved butcher, so my father made a mental note of his opinion and moved on.

The very next night, Dad had his birthday party at his favorite restaurant, Peking Dragon in Dana Point. After finishing his meal, he opened his fortune cookie and got the impression from his fortune that he ought to take his benefits at age 62, just as Butcher Bob had recommended the day before.

After consulting a butcher at Costco and a fortune cookie at Peking Dragon, my father felt he had done as much research on the subject as he could. He decided to take his benefits at 62, not knowing that in 2020, he would still be in great health, going to the gym three times a week, and missing out on tens of thousands of dollars in benefits.

Now, I know that story—true as it is—can seem silly, but I don't mean to mock my father's predicament. At that time, he really didn't have any better resources than what he used. He had nowhere to go for better advice. There were no books in the library or financial planners advertising about Social Security planning. The choice, as far as he could tell, was too complex to solve in any other way. So, he made his choice as well as he could.

Unfortunately, that choice has cost him tens of thousands of dollars in benefits in the years since. And that made it harder for him to maintain his lifestyle throughout retirement.

Learning My Dad's Lessons

Once I realized the mistake my dad had made, I made it a priority to learn enough about Social Security that no client of mine would ever make that poor choice again. I'd let Dad down, and I wasn't about to let anyone else down after him. Dad's story taught me just how important Social Security is to any retirement plan.

In fact, in some cases, if you added up all the numbers, this revenue stream can total over $1 million. That's a lot of money, and it's available to those who paid into the system after they reach retirement age. In other words, if I was going to help people retire, I'd need to master the complexities of Social Security planning and make sure no one was squandering a $1 million income stream on my watch.

So I made sure everyone within my organization became a National Social Security Advisor (NSSA): the certification program that enables you to offer the best possible Social Security advice to clients. To accomplish this goal, my entire staff had to go back to school. We cracked the books, took the exams, and got our NSSA credentials. At the time, this was an incredibly rare credential to hold. I was the 300th person in the country to get this designation, and one of the very first in California.

NSSA SM

NATIONAL SOCIAL SECURITY ADVISORS SM

Of course, being an NSSA doesn't mean I know everything about Social Security planning, but it does mean that I have the resources to answer almost any planning questions. Not only do I understand most of those complex options that boggled Dad's mind, I also have access to the best experts on Social Security in the country. If I can't answer your question, I know who can. I also have the latest software that provides us the latest data and illustrations to make it easier for every one of my clients to make their Social Security choices without consulting fortune cookies and butchers at Costco.

Social Security Is the One Lifeboat Everyone Gets ... and It's the Most Complex

The most important point about Social Security, one it doesn't take an NSSA certificate to realize, is this: You get it, guaranteed, if you paid into the system and meet all the parameters. In this Titanic economy, there's always at least one lifeboat you can jump in. But that lifeboat comes in different sizes depending on when you launch it.

It's hard to overestimate just how important this lifeboat is to retirees. In 2019, the Social Security Administration reported that 45% of all single retired Americans receive 90% of their total retirement income from Social Security. And for almost all the rest, it is still an incredibly valuable resource that can make all the difference in their level of comfort.

In other words, unless you're in that 4% of super-wealthy, getting Social Security right is important.

But there's the rub. While you're guaranteed something from Social Security, you aren't guaranteed all that the program can offer. To maximize Social Security, you need to know when to take it and how to take it.

Unfortunately, Social Security isn't as simple as turning 62, checking a box, and getting a check. Or, rather, it is that simple, if you don't mind missing out on an extra $96,000 in benefits over your lifetime.

If you'd like those extra income benefits, things get complicated very quickly. In fact, there are more than 600 Social Security strategy combinations to choose from. There are more than 2,728 different rules and 2,920 different filing days. That's if you're single. If you're married, there are 5,840 filing days. Each filing day produces a different result. With that many filing days and that many rules, the combination of possible choices becomes paralyzing to the average retiree. Many get frustrated, like my dad, and desperately seek advice in all the wrong places.

In other words, to live your best retirement, you need to maximize this benefit. And to do that, you're going to need some help.

Less and Less Guidance on Social Security

Knowing you'll need some guidance, you might assume you can just go to your local Social Security office and get some help with your forms.

That's a great idea! Here's the problem: Increasingly, that option isn't possible. According to The Associated Press, hundreds of mobile Social Security offices have closed in the last five years.[5] That is a record number of closures, and it is part of a long-term trend. The closing down of Social Security offices has become a bipartisan effort spanning the last few administrations.

Of the offices that still remain open—for now—operational days have been reduced and hours have been cut. This is all happening at the very moment when the largest retirement population on the planet is turning 62. According to the Social Security Administration, last year, 43 million people visited a Social Security field office and half reported waiting more than three weeks to get an appointment. Many had to wait longer than that. Surely, some found out about the length of the wait and never went at all.

Even if you are committed to waiting as long as it takes, you may be disappointed by the guidance you receive from the Social Security employee you speak to. Simply put, these employees are not authorized or equipped to offer counsel or advanced planning

5 And that was before COVID-19. At the moment, all Social Security offices are closed.

advice. Once you sit down for your appointment after waiting three or four weeks, the person on the other side of the desk isn't going to go through those hundreds of options you can choose from. They're just not capable of doing so. It takes too much time, too much knowledge, and too much risk on their part (no one wants to be blamed for giving you the wrong advice).

Instead of giving you this in-person assistance, the administration is encouraging people to access all services online. Now, I will admit, the Social Security website is very good. It's very comprehensive. If you had a few months to dedicate to this decision, you could probably find all the information you would need on that page.

But again, that takes time, and it also takes technological know-how. You can't just ask the webpage to answer your questions. You have to master your computer first.

That can be quite a challenge for those of us reaching or well into our seventh decade. I've been around computers most of my adult life. I got an Atari 64 in 1982. I was part of the Apple Revolution. I use computers every day at work and at home. Yet, I still sometimes need to consult my 9-year-old grandson about how to work my iPad. In other words, unless you have a few free months ahead to prepare for retirement from a career in computer science, getting advice that will affect the rest of your life from a website may be a little intimidating.

Even then, you'll still be at a disadvantage because websites don't make sure you understand what you're reading. There's no human on the other end to double-check your information or make sure you understood the answer correctly. There's no way to describe your very unique financial circumstances or get out-of-the-box advice. There's just a website and a series of complex decisions that determine just how seaworthy your only guaranteed lifeboat will be.

Faced with these difficulties, many would rather just consult the local butcher or start cracking fortune cookies. And I don't blame them.

Why They Make Social Security So Hard

Why on earth would the government want to make it so hard for you to maximize your Social Security benefit?

In a word, money. According to a 2013 study from MarketWatch, 2033 represents a financial cliff after which the government—as it is currently funded—will exhaust its trust fund, which could trigger sharp reductions in benefits.

In other words, Butcher Bob was sort of right about Social Security running out of money. He just had the year and the fund wrong.

The truth is, Social Security wasn't set up to handle our aging population. People are living longer and having fewer children, which has made it much harder to pay for this program. Back in 1935, when the government created Social Security, commonly known as the Old-Age, Survivors, and Disability Insurance (OASDI), they assumed people would only live until 65. The benefit was meant to be used for just a few years.

Now, people like my dad retire at 62 and live on for decades. With people living longer, the government needs more money coming in, but we have just the opposite in this country. Back in 1950, 16 taxpayers supported one Social Security recipient. Today, according to the Mercatus Center, 2.8 taxpayers support one recipient.

The government needs to save money somewhere, and it does so by closing offices and making it far easier to minimize your benefits than to maximize them.

It's all very understandable, but you don't have to be one of the victims of this strategy. It is still possible to get all the money that is coming to you through this program. We just need to walk through all the complexities together.

Chapter 6.

When to Take Social Security

When my father decided to take his Social Security at 62, he assumed it was the best deal he could get. He figured, if he wanted to have time to enjoy the benefits, he should take it earlier.

"If I'm 62 now," he told me right before he made his decision, "and I die when I'm 82, it would be better to take Social Security for 20 years, versus waiting till age 70 and only getting a benefit for 12 years."

Dad expected to live into his late 70s or early 80s. Instead, he's now in his late 80s and showing no signs of slowing down. Now, he wishes he could change that decision, but it's far too late.

The problem was, Dad didn't do the math on retirement the way the Social Security office does. To him, the math said retire now and enjoy what you get for a longer period of time. If he'd done the math the Social Security way, he would have known that taking his benefit at 62 would mean a 25% permanent cut to his monthly check.

Because he got the math wrong, he cost himself 25% of his Social Security income for almost 30 years now.

The worst part about this whole story is that he didn't even need the money. He could have easily kept working a few more years. He was in great health, and he enjoyed his work. He just got some bad advice. And because of that, he took Social Security when he didn't need it and received 25% less when he did. When the time came that he needed more income, we had to find different lifeboats to keep him afloat because his Social Security lifeboat had already set sail.

The Difference a Few Years Make

Obviously, if you can afford it, you don't want to take that big cut in your benefits by taking Social Security too early. But to avoid that cut, you've got to know how long to wait.

Unfortunately, as we learned in the last chapter, knowing the right moment to take Social Security is not an easy question to answer.

I wish I could tell you that there's an easy set date we all have to look for on the calendar, and if we wait that long, we'll maximize every cent we're entitled to. That's not how Social Security works. Instead, the government has staggered the dates when we can receive full benefits. If you were born between 1943 and 1954, you're in luck because your date is pretty easy to remember. Your full retirement age—the date when you can receive full benefits—is 66 on the button. Not a day sooner, not a day later.

But for those of us born after 1954, it gets a little more complicated. For every year past 1954, the government adds two months onto full retirement age. For example, I was born in 1959. My full retirement age is 66 and 10 months. If you were born in 1960, your full retirement age is 67.

Year of birth	Full retirement age (FRA)	Age 62 benefit	FRA benefit	Age 70 benefit
1943–54	66	75.00%	100%	132.00%
1955	66 and 2 months	74.17%	100%	130.67%
1956	66 and 4 months	73.33%	100%	129.33%
1957	66 and 6 months	72.50%	100%	128.00%
1958	66 and 8 months	71.67%	100%	126.67%
1959	66 and 10 months	70.83%	100%	125.33%
1960 & later	67	70.00%	100%	124.00%

Now, this system is subject to change at any time. Just because it's currently set at two months extra for every year after 1954 doesn't mean it will remain that way forever. As we learned in the last chapter, Social Security is expensive, and the government is looking for every way possible to reduce costs. So, you should always keep an eye out for whether the full retirement age jumps up again.

It is entirely conceivable that in the near future, the administration changes policy and says the full retirement age is 68 or 69. Or, they may make you add three months onto each year past 1954 instead of two.

And that means, you need to keep up with policy as it evolves … at least until you take your benefit.

What Happens When You Wait

As of today, full retirement age for people born between 1943 and 1954 is age 66. If you were born during that period and waited to take your benefit when you turn 66, you received 100% of the benefit you were owed. That's quite a bit better than what my dad got.

But that's not all. If you are in good health and feel you can continue working or have other revenue streams to sustain you and allow you to defer your benefit until you are 70, you can actually receive *more* than 100% of your Social Security benefit.

Every year you defer past your full retirement age, you accumulate what is called deferred credits. These add up to a whopping 8% increase on your Social Security benefit each year, up until age 70, when the law essentially requires you to take your benefits, whether you need it or not.

If you defer taking your Social Security past full retirement age for that full four years, you'll end up with as much as 132% of your full retirement Social Security benefit.

This is why my dad really kicks himself. He assumed that if he wanted to enjoy Social Security for 20 years, he'd need to take it at 62. Yet, he ended up costing himself in his monthly and lifetime income.

If my dad was retiring today at 62, he might receive $2,000 a month, for a total of $480,000 by his 82nd birthday. If he'd just waited until he turned 66, he would receive the exact same amount of money, except he'd have been living on $2,500 a month instead of $2,000. And, if he worked until he was 70—as he was perfectly capable of doing—he would receive almost the same amount by 82, except with $3,300 going into his bank account every month.

So, at 82, the only difference for someone like Dad would be how long he worked and how much he received from Social Security per month. However, my dad has lived well past 82, as more and more of us do. At this point, his choice to take his benefit at 62 would mean he would have brought in $624,000. If he'd waited until full retirement, that number would be $660,000. And, if he'd worked until age 70, he'd now have seen $712,800 in Social Security income.

So, Dad, and millions like him, missed out on hundreds per month, and he will end up missing out on tens of thousands in total income over his lifetime, all because he didn't understand how much *when* you take Social Security makes a difference.

When to Take Your Social Security Benefit Early

It is pretty obvious at this point that it is usually in your best financial interest to delay taking your Social Security benefit at least until your full retirement age. The numbers above don't lie: Delaying can make a huge difference in your lifetime benefit amount, assuming you live past age 82.

However, I would never tell you not to take your Social Security benefit at 62. In general, there are two very good reasons why you ought to consider taking Social Security early and not waiting. Reason number one is poor health. If you are in poor health, facing a bad diagnosis, or if few in your family live beyond 75, don't delay another day. Most of the deferment strategies we've looked at thus far have break-even points at age 83. So, if 83 does not look to be in the cards for you, take your benefit earlier rather than later.

The second reason to take Social Security early is: You need the money. If you can't afford to live without Social Security now, take it now. Don't struggle and suffer through the next few years just to increase the value of your monthly income. If you've lost your job or have to provide care for another, then Social Security can offer you the income you need to support and sustain yourself, even if the check could have been larger later.

However, if you are in relatively good health, and if you have no particular financial hardship, waiting can be beneficial in maximizing your Social Security benefits.

But knowing the date you'll take Social Security isn't all you have to concern yourself about. Before you jump ahead to the next lifeboat, we have to consider not just *when* you're taking these benefits, but *how*.

Chapter 7.

How to Take Social Security

Meet John and Mary, two of your fellow passengers on the Titanic economy. John and Mary have done fairly well in their careers, but not quite well enough to be able to expect retirement to be comfortable without a bit of work.

Mary ran her own business, and she has provided about 60% of the family income over the past few decades. John was no slouch, though, working hard as a midlevel manager at his business' corporate office in downtown Los Angeles.

Now, John and Mary are both approaching 66—full retirement age for them—and they're contemplating whether now is the right time to start taking Social Security.

The answer, though, is not quite as simple as just *when* to take their benefit. They also need to consider *how*.

Four Social Security Strategies to Consider

John and Mary could simply take their benefits at 66, but doing so would actually cost them approximately $96,000 in lifetime benefits. There's a better way for them, but it involves using Social Security maximization strategies.

In this book, we'll cover four of the most useful strategies. There are more, but most are not as widely applicable, and some simply don't exist anymore. For example, there was once a strategy called File and Suspend, but the government decided it couldn't afford that one anymore. Millions of Americans were benefiting from File and Suspend, when in April 2016, the past administration removed this strategy overnight. At this point, it's off the table for all retirees. The average couple, using the File and Suspend strategy, was able to increase their monthly benefit amount by an astounding $1,040 per month! That was then; let's focus on now.

There are still plenty of strategies available to maximize your Social Security benefits, and four of the most useful are:

- Spousal Benefit (Restricted Application)
- Do-Over Reset
- Start-Stop-Restart
- Divorce Benefits

These strategies offer people like John and Mary the flexibility they need to get the most from Social Security either as individuals or as a couple.

The Spousal Benefit

For married couples like John and Mary, the spousal benefit can really improve their future financial security.

This is how it works: After reaching full retirement age (which is now a requirement for this strategy), one spouse, in this case John, must first file for Social Security benefits. This allows the other spouse, Mary, to file for a spousal benefit, which is *one-half* of the amount her spouse John is receiving. While receiving a spousal benefit, Mary's own worker benefit increases by 8% per year over the next four years. Upon reaching the age of 70, Mary then can switch to her own worker benefit and begin to enjoy the fruits of four years of 8% deferred credits to her benefit amount. This simple strategy can increase John and Mary's lifetime benefit amount by an astonishing $96,000!

With this benefit, the average couple can increase their monthly income by as much as $640 per month. However, there's a catch: this benefit is only available to those who were 62 or older by January 1, 2016 and can only be activated at full retirement age. If one spouse had been 61-and-364-days-old on New Year's Day, 2016, this strategy wouldn't be available to them.

Now, that doesn't mean the benefit has disappeared for younger people. It just isn't as profitable. The Social Security Administration allows younger spouses to take a spousal benefit, they are just not able to switch to a higher worker benefit at a later date. Luckily for John and Mary, they had both just turned 66 at the right time, so they qualified for the original switching strategy.

Since they qualify, let me show you how the numbers work for John and Mary. At 66, Mary is eligible for $2,000 a month, but if she defers taking Social Security until age 70, she'll get that 32% pay increase, thanks to those 8% deferred credits, and receive $2,640 a month. John, meanwhile, is eligible for $1,600 a month at 66. Now, $1,600 isn't enough for John and Mary's needs, but with the Spousal Benefit, they can combine John's $1,600 when he turns 66 with Mary's spousal benefits of $800 and receive $2,400 per month.

Spousal Benefit Case Study

Mary: Eligible for $2,000 monthly benefit at age 66 or $2,640 at age 70

John: Eligible for $1,600 monthly benefit at age 66

If both claim benefits at age 66, they could receive a total of **$1,036,800** over the next 24 years.

If John claims his benefit at age 66, Mary could claim a spousal benefit of **$800** at age 66.

Then at age 70, Mary could switch to her own maximum monthly worker benefit of **$2,640**.

This strategy could yield a total of **$1,132,800** over 24 years.

That's $96,000 more!

This hypothetical example is used for illustrative purposes only. Actual situations will vary.

So from 66 until 70, John and Mary will have $2,400 coming in from Social Security to cover their expenses. Then, when Mary turns 70, she can switch from a Spousal Benefit—replacing $800 a month with her own maximum monthly worker benefit of $2,640 per month, along with John's own benefit amount of $1,600 per month. Thus, this strategy increases John and Mary's lifetime benefit by more than $96,000!

Do-Over Reset

Let's say John and Mary, like my dad, made a big mistake and took their Social Security benefit too early. They didn't hear about the Spousal Benefit until both of them had started taking Social Security, and now, they feel like they've cheated themselves out of a better retirement.

The government does make some effort to play fair. They recognize that the system is complex and people make mistakes. So, they offer you a way to fix that mistake … if you catch it in time.

So long as John and Mary realize their mistake within the first 12 months of making their original claim for benefits, they can use the once-in-a-lifetime, Do-Over Reset strategy.

Again, this strategy can only be done once and only if it has been a year or less since you made the original claim for benefits. If you are within those parameters, you can fill out a SSA-521 form and repay what you have received to date. You can then put your benefits back into suspension mode, reach full retirement, and then enjoy those wonderful 8% deferred credits.

So, if, after 10 months, Mary decides she'd rather use the Spousal Benefit than take her own benefit, she can fill out the SSA-521 form and pay back the full amount she and John had received. In their case, that would amount to approximately $25,200 (John's FRA of $1,600 and Mary's FRA of $2,000 discounted by 30% for taking benefits at age 62, multiplied by 10 months). That's a lot of money, but if it turns out John and Mary were doing just fine without their benefits, it may be the right choice for them. After all, they could benefit by more than $96,000 over their lifetimes if they pay that money back.

Importantly, exercising the Do-Over Reset option doesn't mean you have to wait to take Social Security until you are 66 or 70. If after paying the full amount back, you realize you have made yet another mistake and need those benefits, the administration will allow you to change your mind for up to 60 days. If at any time within that 60 days you decide you want your benefit or you need the money you repaid back, the government will send you a check for the full value you repaid. Then, you'll start receiving benefits again.

However, once again, you won't be eligible to use this strategy again. So, that second time you start taking benefits—whether within 60 days or not—is the last time you can make the choice.

Start-Stop-Restart

If John and Mary wait just 12 months and one day to apply for a Do-Over Reset, they won't qualify. If they can't afford to pay back that $25,200, they won't qualify, either. However, in that circumstance, all is not lost. There's another strategy called Start-Stop-Restart. This is for a person who wants to pause benefits but doesn't qualify for a Do-Over Reset.

There are plenty of reasons this happens. Sometimes, the cost of paying back Social Security is simply too high to apply for Do-Over Reset. Other times, circumstances simply change after a year or more has passed. Perhaps John lost his job at 62 and didn't expect to work again. He took his benefit to cover his now-missing income. That was fine, but then, John's employer realized how indispensable John was to the company and hired him back at age 64. To really entice him to return to work, they even offered John a raise.

At that point, John would no longer need Social Security, but he also wouldn't qualify for a Do-Over Reset. Even worse, because of his raise, he'd now be penalized for making too much income while on Social Security. For every two dollars John would make above the income threshold, the government would withhold one dollar from his benefit amount.

That would put John in a pretty tough position. He might really want to go back to work for a few more years, but the cost would be pretty high.

That is where the Start-Stop-Restart strategy comes in. This strategy requires no repayment at all. So, John's not out of pocket a penny for filing for this deferment strategy. However, it does require John to continue to receive his benefits until he reaches full retirement age. Then, once John reaches his 66th birthday, both John and Mary can suspend their benefits—if married, both spouses would have to suspend benefits—and those benefits would begin to receive those 8% deferred credits. John and Mary can then elect to restart their Social Security payments at a later date and be the benefactor of a higher monthly amount.

How Divorce Affects Social Security

As I mentioned above, these three strategies are by no means the only ones available. There are Social Security strategies available for many different life circumstances. For instance, there is also a strategy for those who have been divorced.

This strategy is becoming increasingly useful because those retiring today are far more likely to have gone through a divorce than previous—and future—generations. For some reason, the Baby Boomer generation leads the world in divorce. The generation before us mostly just hung in there, and the generation following haven't bothered to get married at nearly the same rate. But our generation, we seem to fall right in the middle: lots of marriage and lots of divorce.

This is not to make light of divorce, but in every crisis, there is an opportunity—and here it is. For those who were married for at least 10 years and divorced for more than two years, Social Security says you are entitled to benefits based on your ex-spouse's work record.

The rule works like this: If half of their benefit is more than all of yours, you get half of theirs. Now, don't worry about them.

You aren't actually taking their money. They still get the full amount of their benefit, but you can claim the Spousal Benefit and get the same deal John and Mary had above.

I like to call this the Dirty Rat Strategy. Let me explain why.

A couple of years ago, I was conducting a dinner seminar in Cerritos. I explained this benefit to the audience, and when I looked up from my slide presentation, I saw a woman thrashing about in the back of the room.

She was fairly far away, and I thought she may be having a medical emergency. So, I asked, "Ma'am, are you okay?"

"I'm doing fantastic!" she yelled back.

"Well, ma'am, could you tell me why you are thrashing around back there?"

This woman literally stood up on her chair and yelled at the top of her lungs, "You mean to tell me, Mark, if I was married to a person for 10 years and divorced for more than two that I qualify for half of their Social Security benefits?"

"That's how it works," I replied.

"Then, the reason I'm jumping around is because I was married to someone for 36 years—whom I'll affectionately refer to as Dirty Rat. He treated me poorly, but he made a lot of money, and today, he's probably receiving about $3,000 a month. So, you're telling me, Mark, if he's making $3,000 a month, I qualify for $1,500?"

"Again, that's how it works."

Then she became even more excited. "Right now, I'm only making $900 a month, and you just told me I qualify for $600 more a month because of that dirty rat ex of mine! You've made my day!"

This woman was so excited at this point that, after the seminar, she followed me to my car and wanted to do a consultation in the parking lot. I had to inform her that I didn't do parking lot consultations, but I was happy to see her at her soonest convenience.

She showed up at the office the very next day. I sat with her, and we did a little research on her dirty rat. Unfortunately, we discovered that her dirty rat had not only cheated on her, he had actually cheated on the federal government, as well. Even though he had made a lot of money, he had earned it all under the table and hadn't paid taxes on it. As a result, he was only earning $500 a month from Social Security.

Despite deserving the benefits of this strategy as much as any of my clients, she didn't qualify. But she's an exception. Almost always, if one former spouse made vastly more than the other, then this is a strategy worth looking into. The rule of thumb is this: If half of theirs is more than all of yours, this could be a strategy that works well for you!

In fact, if you have been divorced multiple times and were married for the designated periods of time, you can use this strategy with whichever ex-spouse receives the largest benefit. Although, it is important to realize, you can only use this with one ex-spouse at a time.

Knowledge Makes All the Difference

The bottom line with Social Security is that it's an incredible benefit, a lifeboat for all, but it can be complicated. There are countless rules and thousands of filing days, and each filing day and strategy selected produces a different result for your monthly and lifetime income.

Simply contemplating all those choices is almost impossible. In fact, a group of engineers figured out that if you took all 2,728 different rules and overlaid it with all 5,840 filing days, the combinations of choices relating to Social Security could exceed 100 million. Those possibilities are literally impossible to imagine!

Facing such odds, it's easy to despair. How on earth could anyone possibly make the best choice out of 100 million? Well, the answer is they couldn't—at least, not on their own. If you try to handle this process alone, you're more likely than not to make mistakes like my dad did.

The only way to overcome this problem is through the use of technology and expertise. That's why I will provide anyone who reads this book with a 22-page custom Social Security analysis and strategy report. To get it, just go to www.accessretirementgroup.com, click on Social Security Planning on the home page, and fill out the information required.

Within those pages, you'll see what your financial future looks like if you take benefits early or use a particular strategy. If you want to maximize your benefit, it gives you that information, too. This report uses the most advanced technology available to sort through those millions of possible combinations of strategies and dates to give you the basic options before you.

That way, when you finally get a meeting at a Social Security office, you won't walk in hoping they can guide you to the right choice. You'll already have the answers. You can simply tell them, "I want to do this. I know that this is the best option for me."

That's the best way to handle the Social Security office. They are excellent at following through with your instructions. That's what they're really there for. When you want guidance, you come to someone like me. When you know the benefit you want, you go to them.

With the help of an advisor—or even just this 22-page book—you can make the best Social Security choice for you.

But what about all those other options? How can you make such a big choice without truly understanding the whole system? I understand that hesitation, but you don't have to master every aspect of Social Security to receive the maximized benefits. Think of Social Security like electricity. You don't need to know how electricity works to utilize it. You don't need to understand what an electron or a neutron is or how electricity gets from the power station to the plug in your wall. All you need to know for your purposes is that when you flip a switch, the light turns on. You can get all the benefits of electricity in your home with that simple information. You can leave the rest of the complexity to experts like electricians and physicists.

So, leave the complexity of Social Security to people like me and my team. All you need is the 22-page report and an appointment with me. Then, you can go to your nearest Social Security office and maximize this lifeboat to carry you off into retirement.

Lifeboats Beyond the Underutilized

I know that, for many of you, the advice in this section may have come too late. You may have taken your Social Security benefit early, and you've passed the point where you could correct for that choice.

Others among you, no matter how you handled Social Security, find the benefit isn't sufficient for your needs.

Others still will need to discover other sources of income to live on while they wait for their Social Security to reach its maximum value with all those deferred credits.

So, for now, let's leave behind the Social Security lifeboat, and let's head on down the deck to your unused-but-available lifeboat related to your retirement savings.

Part III

Your Unused-but-Available Lifeboat

Chapter 8.

It's Time to Worry About the Market

My clients often tell me,[6] "Mark, I'm not that worried about Social Security. To be honest with you, I've been very smart with my finances. I've put my money away in the market, and now that I'm retiring, I expect I'll be very well taken care of by that income."

What they're talking about, of course, is their retirement plans, usually an IRA, 401(k), or 403(b).

Invariably, I congratulate these clients on their smart planning. Then, I tell them, "It's wonderful that you've prepared so well for retirement, but retirement isn't as simple as living on your IRA. There's more to this process—and far more risk—than you're aware of."

I don't like spoiling people's day, but this is something everyone needs to hear. If you have money in the market, you have a lot of decisions to make. And as we learned in the first part of this book, you need to start making those decisions soon.

6 Or at least they used to, before COVID-19.

Distribution Rules

Before you can really understand where to place your money before we hit the iceberg, we need to talk about the position your money is in now. When you are retiring, there are two main concerns you have to address with your retirement account.

The first is about distribution rules and the second is distribution methods.

Distribution rules can be rather boring and complicated—and they're constantly changing. The Secure Act of 2019, for instance, just recently changed many of the rules relating to your qualified retirement plans. So I'm not going to spend a lot of time on them right now. Instead, I'll give you the highlights in the form of two easy-to-remember rules: the *can't* and the *must* rule.

The *can't* rule says that if you have a qualified plan—which all IRA, 401(k), and 403(b) plans are—you *can't* touch it until you're 59 1/2. If, for some reason, you do need to touch that money, you're going to encounter in most cases something called an "excise penalty." That penalty amounts to a 10% fee that's added on top of the tax that you would pay for any money you take out of your account. So if you really need that $50,000 from your IRA before you are 59 1/2, you'll not only pay tax on that $50,000, but you'll also pay an additional $5,000 as an excise penalty.

Now, there's nothing you can do about the tax, whenever you take this money out. That tax is part of what makes this a "qualified" account. You put the money in as a tax-deductible contribution, so now, you owe that tax back to the government. When the money was growing, it grew tax deferred, but when you pull the money out, it is all going to be taxable. But once you pass the *can't* rule age, you won't have to deal with additional penalties.

Why is there a *can't* rule at all? Because this money is meant to be for your retirement. That's the whole purpose of the account. The money has been earmarked for when you reach retirement age. If you access it sooner, that means you haven't kept your end of the bargain for the benefits of the policy. Hence the penalty.

The *must* rule refers to the other possible misuse of your retirement plan. Let's say, instead of needing that $50,000, you haven't needed your plan at all. You've gone through the whole of your 60s continuing to work and earning enough to get by.

Well, the government wants to get the tax revenue on your retirement policy at some point. They aren't going to allow you to just hold on to all that income tax-free forever. So they created the *must* rule. The new Secure Act of 2019 states that you *must* begin to take distributions by April 1 of the year following your 72nd birthday. After you blow out the candles on that 72nd birthday cake, you will have until April 1 of the following year to start taking RMDs, or required minimum distributions. If you don't, you'll be facing penalties again. That penalty would amount to 50% of your RMD. For example, if your RMD was $2,000 for the 2019 tax year and you failed to take it, the penalty would be $1,000.

However, so long as you comply with the *can't* and *must* rules, you can begin taking out money any time without penalty.

Distribution Methods

Far more interesting than distribution rules are distribution methods. When you retire, if you are leaving a larger company, you will probably sit down with someone from HR and listen to the methods for distributing your retirement plan income.

The person in HR will place several options out in front of you. Option number one is to **stay put**. This is a very popular choice because, essentially, it means nothing changes. The HR person will say to you something like, "We've been managing your money for the last 37 years, and we would be delighted to manage your money for the next 30 years. As you know from your statements, we've been successful with your account so far. If you stay put, we will continue to employ the same strategies we did for you since you started this plan in your 20s. You can then expect to keep seeing these same returns into your 90s."

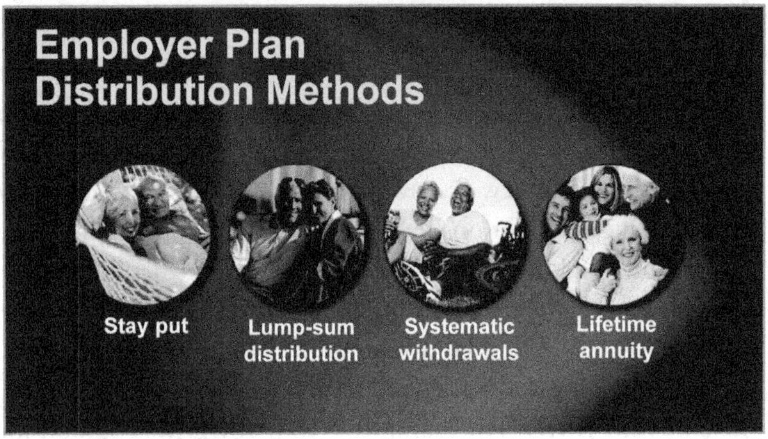

Again, this is a very popular choice among those preparing to retire, and for obvious reasons. This option sounds very attractive on the surface. However, as we'll see, it's not nearly as rosy as HR might make it sound.

Option two is far less popular. It's called a **lump-sum distribution**. Not many people choose this one because it can amount to tax suicide for your retirement funds. With this option, you get your whole retirement account value in a single lump sum. That might sound great at first, but remember, you'll have to pay taxes on the entire account value when your taxes are due.

There are rare circumstances when a lump-sum distribution may be useful. If, for instance, you have only a small amount in your retirement account and that money could be used to pay off a loan or mortgage, it may be worth paying the tax and removing that debt burden before you begin your retirement years. However, in most cases, this is the least desirable option.

The next option that most HR people give you is called **systematic withdrawals**. This allows you to begin taking withdrawals from your plan immediately, so you can enjoy your retirement and live in comfort.[7]

With systematic withdrawals, your remaining account value will still be managed by the same people as before—just like with the **stay-put option**—but you'll start taking some of that money out every month to cover the missing income from your job.

Now, something HR may not highlight for you is that these systematic withdrawals are regularly recalculated based on what is in your account—which is connected to the market—so you should expect some good years and some bad years and a reasonable amount of volatility in your withdrawals.

If the volatility of payments in systematic withdrawals bothers you, then some people opt for the final HR-approved option, which is the **lifetime annuity option**. This option converts your entire balance into a stream of payments. These payments will remain steady instead of changing with the value of the account as it fluctuates in the market.

However, the lifetime annuity—sometimes called immediate annuity—does have some drawbacks. First and foremost, this decision is irrevocable. Once you choose to convert to an immediate annuity, there is no way to go back and convert the annuity back to the old IRA. You are essentially deciding to take your money as a lump sum, only receiving it over your life expectancy instead of all at once. If you live beyond normal life expectancy, you will have no money left to leave to a beneficiary. And if you

7 Remember, you'll have to take these withdrawals by no later than April 1 of the year following your 72nd birthday.

die with money still in the account—and you don't have a beneficiary designation—the remaining balance goes to those managing your account, not your family. So, if you choose this option, that beneficiary designation is very important if you want the remaining money to go to your spouse or other beneficiary. With that in place, he or she would receive either a lump sum or income from your annuity for the remainder of their life (or until the funds run out, at which point, all payments would stop).[8]

An equally negative aspect of the lifetime annuity is the lack of flexibility with your funds. You set up at the beginning that you will receive a certain withdrawal every month, and you cannot change that, no matter what you do.

If you have $1,000,000 in your account and get $50,000 a year, you can't decide next year that you now want $100,000 so you can buy a boat. There's no extra money and zero flexibility. You get what you get each month, and that's it.

Again, this is an irrevocable decision. It would be the equivalent of getting on a 1,000-mile bridge over water. Once you're on that bridge, there are no exits. The only option is to go forward. So make sure this is what you want before you make this choice. It does provide an income stream that you cannot outlive, which is a good thing, but it limits your liquidity options. There are no other options except to receive income for life. That's it.[9]

8 You may also be able to leave the principal to your children. However, such provisions will reduce your monthly income.

9 It's important to note that the Secure Act of 2019 now allows for companies under ERISA's (Employee Retirement Income Security Act, established in 1974) Safe Harbor guidelines to provide other annuity options within their corporate plans to better meet consumer needs. However, there are still limits in the options they can provide you.

Don't Stay Put on the Titanic's Deck

There are costs and benefits to all these options, but there's one in particular I want to focus on here: staying put.

Staying put is often the preferred choice for many new retirees. After all, the arguments laid out above are compelling. Over the last few decades, you have watched your IRA, 401(k), or 403(b) account grow, so why not follow the same strategy into retirement? This option provides the ultimate peace of mind. The money will keep growing, and you don't have to worry about it. You have the flexibility to withdraw money when you need it, and switch over to systematic withdrawals when the time is right.

All you have to do is keep checking your balance when it arrives in the mail—just as you have since you were in your 20s—and enjoy seeing the numbers grow.

Yet, staying put is often a mistake for retired people. The fact is, you are no longer in your 20s. Your needs are different, and this option can fall dramatically short when financial seas begin to grow more turbulent.

In many circumstances, staying put can be like standing around on the deck of the Titanic, enjoying the fresh air while the ship heads toward that iceberg. Instead of taking the time to get into a lifeboat early before the crash comes, you're doing nothing, waiting for disaster to strike.

Chapter 9.

Sequence of Returns Risk

The real reason staying put could be a challenge for some retirees is because of the **sequence of returns risk**. Don't feel bad if you haven't heard of this before. Most people don't know what it means. I do between 30 and 40 seminars on this topic a year, and almost no one ever raises their hands when I ask about this concept. Yet, sequence of returns risk can determine if your lifeboat is going to stay afloat or if it will sink into those icy seas.

So what is it? And why do you want to do everything in your power to avoid it?

Sequence of returns risk refers to when you begin taking distributions from your retirement account. If you decide to stay put and continue to trust the market, your whole future depends on what happens at the point you stop accumulating and start withdrawing.

Timing Matters in Money and Romance

The best and easiest way to understand just how consequential sequence of returns risk can be to your future is through story. So let me tell you a little something about my wife and me.

My wife, Cathy, and I have been married for 37 years. We were college sweethearts, and we have four children and nine grandkids (and counting). Our last child left the family home permanently in 2016, leaving us with the whole place to ourselves for the first time in decades.

While I know not everyone agrees, for me, being an empty nester is wonderful. It almost feels like Cathy and I are dating again. The kids are gone. They're off living their own lives, freeing us up to just take care of us. We no longer have to live under the limitations raising kids put on our marriage.

So, in 2016, when Cathy and I were in the first months of empty nester elation, I said to her one rainy afternoon, "I need to go to Staples to pick up a filing cabinet. Do you want to come with me?" The response she gave me was almost as enthusiastic as I might expect if I had asked her to go to Maui for the weekend.

"I would love to go to Staples with you to pick up a filing cabinet!" she said. Of course, she was never that enthusiastic about such a trip when the kids were around, but somehow, even that mundane trip seemed like an adventure, now that just the two of us were doing it.

She jumped in the car before I could even get my keys. We were thrilled to be together, driving off to Staples in the rain. Even the weather outside wasn't enough to dampen our enjoyment of the big event. On the way to Staples, Cathy got a bright idea.

"Mark, why don't you drop me off at Ralphs, next door to Staples? I can pick up some amazing food, and we can enjoy a candlelit dinner when we get back. Just like old times. You get the filing cabinet, I'll get the food, and we'll head home and cook it together."

That sounded like a marvelous plan to me. So I dropped Cathy off at Ralphs, and right on time, I entered Staples where I was scheduled to meet with Joey, a sales assistant who was assigned by store management to put my heavy fireproof filing cabinet into our vehicle.

It all went wrong from there. The person at the register informed me that Joey wasn't available to help with my filing cabinet.

"He's on break," the cashier told me.

"That's fine," I said, my mood still unperturbed. "How long will he be?"

"He's scheduled to be back in an hour."

"An hour?" I exclaimed. I didn't have that kind of time. "Can you help me instead?"

"I can't leave the register. And there's no one else here who is qualified to help. All I can do is offer you a handcart. You're certainly welcome to try to load your filing cabinet on your own. Otherwise, it'll be an hour before someone can assist you."

I really didn't want to wait an hour. So I decided to try lifting that heavy filing cabinet onto a handcart and loading it myself. With great difficulty and after several exhausting, back-breaking tries that involved hitting my head on the liftgate of my SUV, I managed to get the cabinet into my vehicle in the pouring rain. By the time I was done, I was soaking wet, exhausted, and extremely irritated.

I slammed the liftgate, jumped into my car, and drove home. When I got home, it was still pouring, and I discovered, much to my further annoyance, that Cathy wasn't there to help me, either. I had to unload that same filing cabinet all on my own.

Suddenly, I wished a few of the kids were still at home to lend a hand. Instead, I had to do it all by myself.

With a backache, an emerging headache, and a whole lot of exasperation, I installed the filing cabinet in my office and began putting my documents into place.

An hour went by when I heard a knock at the front door. I thought to myself: *Who's knocking on my door in the middle of a storm?* To my surprise, the answer was Cathy.

She looked like she'd been through a car wash. She was holding two bags of food, and she was livid.

I said to her in astonishment, "Cathy, where have you been?"

She looked at me with as much surprise as anger, saying, "Mark, you left me at Ralphs holding two bags of food in a rainstorm. Fortunately for you, a neighbor saw me, picked me up, and brought me home."

"I'm so upset with you right now. You can forget that meal I was going to cook with you. In fact, you might as well get used to going to McDonald's from here on out."

She dropped the food at my feet and stormed upstairs. I just stood there. I felt as if I was awaking from a nightmare. Once I recovered from the initial shock, I went back to my office, sat down, and began to look on the internet for sites giving information on early signs of dementia.

I was sitting there, still in utter disbelief about what I had just done, when, about an hour later, Cathy came down to my office. She stood over my desk, looked me in the eyes, and said, "Mark, I forgive you."

I was so shocked by her declaration that I asked her, "You what?" To which she replied again, "I forgive you!" I told her how sorry I was about 15 times over. I walked around my desk; I gave her a big hug. We laughed, we kissed, and we made up. And Cathy, in fact, offered to make me dinner that same night.

During dinner, I became extremely curious why Cathy was so quick to forgive me after the boneheaded move that I pulled that afternoon.

She told me, "Mark, prior to that boneheaded move, I had experienced about 35 blissful years of marriage with you. In fact, to speak in a language you really understand, you had put so many deposits into our marriage's emotional bank account that on the date of this blunder, your account balance happened to be so positive that even leaving me in the rain holding two bags of food was not going to blow the deal."

But before I could pat myself on the back and celebrate a little bit, Cathy said, "Not so fast, Mark. Had you pulled this stunt on me following our first date in college, you would be eating this dinner with an entirely different girl right now. If you had done this to me back then, I would have dropped you flat."

Here's the moral to that story. Bad things can happen, even to good people. But the order, the timing, or the *sequence* of those bad things makes all the difference in the world.

You blow a first date, you're done. You don't get date number two. You do something stupid after 35 years of blissful marriage, and you'll usually work it out.

Your retirement account works the same way. If the Titanic economy hits an iceberg in the 30th year of your blissful retirement with robust returns, you're probably going to get through it. But if the Titanic economy hits that iceberg in the first couple of years of taking distributions from your retirement account, you may be going down with the ship.

Bob and Jim Encounter Sequence of Returns Risk

Let me introduce you to Bob and his friend, Jim. Bob and Jim had very similar careers, making just about the same amount of money and putting aside the same amount into their 401(k)s. The only difference between them is when they retired. Bob retired 30 years ago, and Jim is retiring now.

When Bob retired at 66, he had about $1,000,000 in his 401(k). He decided to stay put and set up systematic withdrawals of 5% a year. That came out to $50,000 a year, which Bob felt was plenty for his needs.

Fortunately for Bob, the first year of his retirement, the market returned 5% on his plan. The next year was a positive 28%. In year number three, Bob was able to receive a 22% return on investment. Year number four, he got -5%. And for the most part, the rest of those early years followed a similar pattern, with only a few modest losses along the way.

Fast-forwarding to year 25, and you'll see that Bob experienced a blowout, a major market correction in which he lost 25% of his portfolio. But because that negative event happened 25 years into his retirement— following years and years of prosperity and positive returns—Bob was still able to continue to receive his $50,000 every year. Overall, Bob saw an average of 6% returns, and because of the timing of the big swings in his returns, he lived out his retirement in comfort. In fact, when he died, he was able to leave his heirs approximately $2.5 million, all because good things happened early for Bob in the distribution phase.

Things didn't work out so well for Jim. In fact, his 25 years of retirement saw the exact opposite trends in the market. Instead of seeing that positive 5% return in his first year of retirement, it didn't occur until year 25. And instead of losing 25% in year 25, that loss hit in the first year of his retirement. Jim still saw the same 6% average return over his entire retirement, but because the bad times hit early, his money didn't even reach those big increases late in his life.

	"Up" Market—Bob			"Down" Market—Jim		
Age	5% Annual Withdrawals	Annual Return	Year-End Value	5% Annual Withdrawals	Annual Return	Year-End Value
65			$1,000,000			$1,000,000
66	$50,000	5%	$1,000,000	$50,000	-25%	$700,000
67	$50,000	28%	$1,230,000	$50,000	-14%	$552,000
68	$50,000	22%	$1,450,600	$50,000	-10%	$446,800
69	$50,000	-5%	$1,328,070	$50,000	16%	$468,288
70	$50,000	20%	$1,543,684	$50,000	21%	$516,628
71	$50,000	19%	$1,786,984	$50,000	5%	$492,460
72	$50,000	23%	$2,147,990	$50,000	-16%	$363,666
73	$50,000	9%	$2,291,309	$50,000	8%	$342,760
74	$50,000	16%	$2,607,919	$50,000	14%	$340,746
75	$50,000	23%	$3,157,740	$50,000	24%	$372,525
76	$50,000	22%	$3,802,443	$50,000	14%	$374,679
77	$50,000	-26%	$2,763,808	$50,000	5%	$343,412
78	$50,000	-15%	$2,299,237	$50,000	-15%	$241,901
79	$50,000	5%	$2,364,199	$50,000	-26%	$129,006
80	$50,000	14%	$2,645,186	$50,000	22%	$107,388
81	$50,000	24%	$3,230,031	$50,000	23%	$82,087
82	$50,000	14%	$3,632,235	$50,000	16%	$45,221
83	$50,000	8%	$3,872,814	$50,000	9%	$0
84	$50,000	-16%	$3,203,164	$50,000	23%	$0
85	$50,000	5%	$3,313,322	$50,000	19%	$0
86	$50,000	21%	$3,959,120	$50,000	20%	$0
87	$50,000	16%	$4,542,579	$50,000	-5%	$0
88	$50,000	-10%	$4,038,321	$50,000	22%	$0
89	$50,000	-14%	$3,422,956	$50,000	28%	$0
90	$50,000	-25%	$2,517,217	$50,000	5%	$0
Average Return		**6%**			**6%**	

Nothing separated the careers or financial choices of Bob and Jim. Both had successfully saved a million dollars toward their retirement. Both took 5% systematic withdrawals and decided to stay put with the rest. Both saw an average of 6% positive return on their money over their retirement. Yet, because of sequence of returns risk, one lived comfortably and left millions to his heirs, and the other ran out of money years earlier than expected.

Are You at Risk Today?

After reading Bob's and Jim's story, there is an obvious question you must ask yourself: What is the probability of the sequence of returns risk impacting your retirement? Is it high? Is it low?

Or, put another way: Are negative returns eminent? Are positive returns going to continue well into the future?

Your first instinct might be to assume you'll be looking at Bob's ledger for your retirement. After all, the economy has been strong for years now. You might hope to see some big returns in the near future.

That's certainly possible, but for my money, I'll check with the experts. And there's no bigger expert than Warren Buffett.

As we covered in Chapter 2, Buffett has run the numbers, and he believes we are due for a huge correction very soon. While it looks like clear sailing today, we are heading into dangerous waters very quickly. We're even more overvalued now than we were in March 2000,[10] and the result of that correction? A 47% loss 34 months later. What would your portfolio look like if we suffered another loss like that next year?

The truth is, we're not living in Bob's economy anymore. You can't expect 6% or 7% every year, and you have to expect a correction at every turn.

If you choose to stay put with your money right now, you are gambling on the hope that, somehow, we're going to be able

10 Or we were, prior to the COVID-19 correction. How significant the ultimate drop will be is yet to be determined.

to steer our way through the most overvalued market in recent history. Unfortunately, the far more likely result is that there's an iceberg ahead. You may not see it right now, but it's just over the horizon. So, are you in a position to get off the boat when the time comes? Or are you still thinking staying put is the best idea?

Chapter 10.

Five Ways to Maximize Space on Your Unused Lifeboat

In the last two chapters, I laid out why it may not always be best to stay put and risk your savings by keeping it invested in this Titanic economy. The risk is too high, and the chance of a correction is too great to trust your retirement to the market.

But what are you supposed to do? Your Social Security lifeboat will help, but it may not be enough for your needs. That lifeboat may prove too small for your financial requirements, particularly if the surf gets very rough in the years ahead.

Luckily, there's another big lifeboat on board. This one is widely available to anyone who has a retirement plan—but it's rarely used. That rarity of use is particularly unfortunate because, in many ways, this is your best lifeboat option. Using the right strategies, you can expand the size, fill any holes, and make sure it stays afloat no matter what is ahead.

So useful is this lifeboat that it comes with five safety nets that can protect you while maximizing value to last you throughout retirement, no matter how long that is or what is happening to the economy.

Right now, this lifeboat is just sort of sitting over there on the side of the deck, completely ignored while everyone is rushing about, looking for a way off this Titanic ship we're all on. You don't need to lose your head or try to cram into the Social Security lifeboat like the rest.

Instead, let's head over and see if this lifeboat might meet your financial needs.

Safety Net #1: Annual Reset

Perhaps the greatest value of this lifeboat is that it gives you some of the benefits of the market without any of the risk. It removes risk by insulating your account against the violent swings of the economy.

And that insulation starts with the **annual reset safety net**. Annual reset is very simple: Whatever your account earns on the market over the course of a year, you get to keep. There are no givebacks. In other words, all your gains from the past year are locked in, even if the market plummets the next day.

Now, there's a downside. In exchange for keeping all past gains and capping your losses at 0%, you have to give up some upside potential. Some plans cap earnings by crediting only 50% of the gains in a selected market index. Other plans, designed more for maximizing income, apply a hard annual cap of 4% to the account. Other plans deduct a spread or margin of 3.25% from annual index gains. In each circumstance, market potential is capped in exchange for having all gains locked in and eliminating negative returns. Essentially, plans can be structured to maximize growth, maximize lifetime income, or a little bit of both, but there's always some give-and-take.

Sound like a bad deal? After all, in an indexed mutual fund, when the market goes up 60%, you get all of that increase. Who wants to settle for 30% when you can get double? But that thinking only works when you're sailing in clear waters or when you're not taking systematic withdrawals. Because otherwise, the price of realizing all those market gains is you assuming the risk for all the losses. So when the market drops 50%, you could lose 50% as well. Couple a 50% loss with a systematic withdrawal of 5%, and you've got a sinking ship.

To really see the benefit of the annual reset, we've got to do some quick math. Take a look at the chart below:

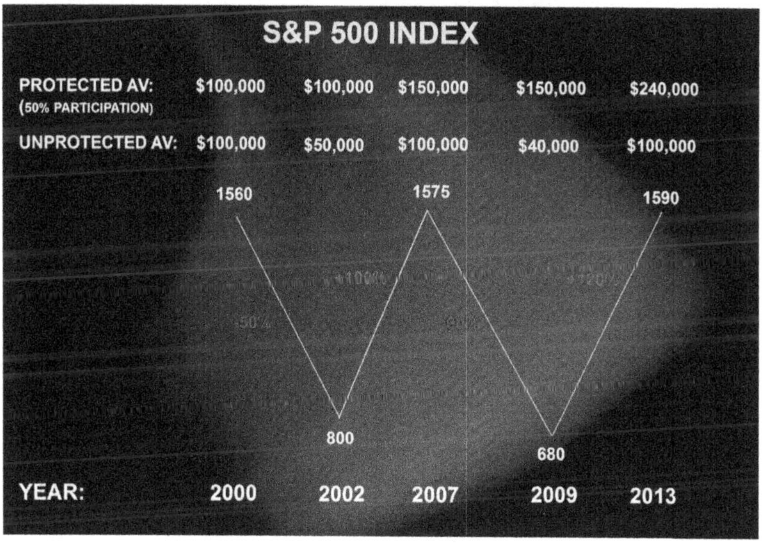

As you can see, while a standard unprotected IRA account keeps its gains, it also loses value with the market. On the other hand, with the safety net of annual reset, your account value stays the same, because all gains are locked in. So when the market index recovers all past losses, your IRA would only regain its initial value, while your account with annual reset gets half those gains to the tune of $50,000 added to the previous balance.

During a 13-year period from 2000 to 2013 on the previous chart, the account holder with annual reset earns an extra $140,000, with $240,000 total in the account. Compare that to the IRA that earned nothing. It ended up at zero gain for the account holder over that 13-year period. Slow and steady—coupled with annual reset—wins the race!

With our Titanic economy heading toward an iceberg, do you really want to risk everything just so you can make all those hypothetical gains that may never materialize?

Take one more close look at that chart. Now, does half the gains and none of the losses still sound like a bad deal? I bet not.

Safety Net #2: Guaranteed Roll-Up Rates

Maybe the annual reset safety net doesn't sound good enough to you. You need to see profits in your account, no matter what. You need your money to be increasing every year, or it won't last.

I've got great news for you: this lifeboat has another safety net for you: the **guaranteed roll-up**. With this safety net, some plans during the accumulation phase guarantee you up to 7.5% compounded annually for 10 years into your income account value. So even if we go through an extended period of losses in the market, your income account value will still be growing, no matter what.

Even better, if the market exceeds 7.5% growth, you get half the value of those market increases. Whichever account performs better, that's the base number you'll use to determine your monthly benefits in the future.

Combine that with the annual reset, and you essentially not only avoid all losses but guarantee reasonable gains in your account. And, if we see a huge spike in the market, you still get 50% of those increases.

Safety Net #3: Up-Front Bonus

Safety net #3 is an even more straightforward bargain for the account holder. For this, you don't even need the math we did with the first two options. Basically, if you jump ship and switch over to this lifeboat, you can get a bonus for making that transition. Some companies, in fact, will add up to 30% or $30,000 onto your initial deposit of $100,000 and reflect that bonus in your income account value.

Would an extra $30,000 in your income account value help you stay afloat over the coming decades? Then this is definitely worth considering.

Safety Net #4: Income for Life

The first three safety nets all help boost the balance of your income account value, but what about when you need to start taking those systematic withdrawals?

Perhaps the biggest concern for anyone looking at their retirement account is whether it's going to run out of money. You don't want your lifeboat to get you halfway home only to spring a leak and sink.

In an unprotected account, it's entirely possible to simply run out of money. When your principal hits zero in an unprotected IRA, for instance, your withdrawals hit zero. You just stop getting checks in the mail, and it's up to you to find a way to fill the hole in your finances.

Safety net #4 ensures that can't happen. This safety net guarantees that you will always get an established 5% (more or less, depending on your age) withdrawal amount from your income account value for the rest of your life. Forget the market. Forget the account balance. You'll get an approximate 5% withdrawal based upon your income account value—no matter what else happens—for your life AND the life of your spouse, if you're married.

That 5% is calculated once and is based upon the balance in the income account value at the moment you start taking systematic withdrawals. So, if you have $246,000 in your income account value at age 72, and the withdrawal factor for that age is 5%, you'll get 5% of $246,000 per year for the rest of your life. No matter what happens to your account, you can expect $1,025 to arrive monthly, even if your principal balance hits zero.

You can't outlive this safety net. Even if you live to 130 and become the oldest person in the world, you won't outlive this income stream. And, if you set this safety net up right, this income stream can actually last even longer. If your spouse outlives you and hits 139, they can benefit from this income source for the full duration of their life, as well.

Safety Net #5: Income Doubler for Long-Term Care

Let me ask you an important question that too often never gets asked: Do you have long-term care insurance? I doubt it. According to the Insurance Library, only 10% of all retired Americans have some form of long-term care insurance. The reason no one asks you about it is because it is not practical for most people. It's simply too expensive and too hard to get. Many retirees can't even qualify for it.

But that doesn't mean you can't benefit from policies similar to long-term care insurance. In fact, this lifeboat has just such a policy: Safety net #5. With this safety net, your income from this lifeboat will *double* as soon as you cannot perform two out of the six activities of daily living.

These are basic activities like eating and moving around. When those become too difficult, and you need to pay for assistance—or rely on a loved one who has to sacrifice work to provide you care—your income can double to accommodate that help.

Whether it's help from family, at-home care, or an assisted living facility, getting help with your impairment will be expensive.

To help you pay for it, that $1,025 a month you were receiving before will become $2,050 a month until the account value is depleted to zero. At which point, it will revert back to the original payment amount on a lifetime basis. That way, you can afford the assistance you need to deal with your circumstances.[11]

A Lifeboat for All Weather

Whether the economy is strong or weak, growing or shrinking, you need a retirement lifeboat that can see you through your whole retirement.

With these safety nets, your balance will grow no matter what, and at a rate that will allow you that extra comfort and security you need. You'll never run out of money, and you'll have more coming to you when you need it most.

There is a lifeboat that can sail through any storm and includes all of the safety nets discussed thus far. All that's left is to tell you the name of that lifeboat.

11 The average long-term care impairment period is around two years.

Chapter 11.

The Fixed Indexed Annuity Lifeboat

In Chapter 1, I related how I entered into retirement planning. At the time, I was helping wealthy real estate investors with property acquisitions. Then, one of my clients told me they had found an amazing retirement plan, the same one, in fact, that my father had just discovered.

The opportunity that was able to attract both a super-wealthy investor and my dad was an earlier version of an insurance product known as a **fixed indexed annuity**. And, in fact, the retirement account that I just described in the last chapter is the exact same type of annuity.

Now, before you close the book and shout at the walls about how much you hate annuities, the fixed indexed annuity is not like the other annuities you've heard about. This product has all the advantages and security that I described previously, and it really can provide that comfort and stability you are looking for.

Annuities Are Not All the Same

There's a reason I delayed naming this product until this point in the book. There's a lot of prejudice against annuities out there, and often, there's good reason for that. However, not all annuities are created equal, and while your feelings may be completely justified for some annuities, they're misplaced here.

There is a great deal of difference between the various kinds of annuities. Take, for instance, the lifetime annuity we covered in Chapter 8. That's one of the popular options people are offered when retiring, but a lifetime annuity has all those downsides we covered before. You lose control of your money. You have no flexibility. And, if you're not careful, whatever is left when you die will go to those managing your account, not your family. That's the 1,000-mile bridge over water with no exits option, and I think there's a better way.

Another option is the variable annuity. These are probably the annuities you've heard the most about and heard you should avoid. A variable annuity is tied to the performance of the stock market or investments you've selected. This means there's far more volatility and risk involved when investing your money here. You can receive the protective safety nets described in Chapter 10 with a variable annuity—but at a significantly higher cost. How high? They can be above 4%, which severely decreases your potential gains—often the big selling point for these accounts—and the guarantees are frequently lower than the fixed indexed annuity.

If the lifetime annuity is a 1,000-mile bridge with no exits, you can think of the variable annuities as a toll road. It has its benefits, but it comes with multiple expenses and high annual fees.

In contrast to both of those annuity options, the fixed indexed annuity provides all the benefits of the last chapter, plus far more flexibility and security. The fixed indexed annuity could be compared to taking the 101 from LA to San Francisco.

Additional Benefits of a Fixed Indexed Annuity

The fixed indexed annuity gives you all of those safety net benefits we covered in the previous chapter: the annual reset, guaranteed roll-up, up-front bonus, income for life, and income doubler for long-term care. Those, in and of themselves, make this one of the most consumer-friendly annuities on the market today—and I'd argue, one worth considering for retirement income.

And they aren't even the whole story. With a fixed indexed annuity, you also have far more flexibility with your principal. We've already talked about how you can't change your systematic withdrawals on your lifetime annuity after they're set. There's no principal to draw from anymore. But that's not the case with a fixed indexed annuity. If you decide you want to buy a boat when you're 75, you can do that with a fixed indexed annuity.[12]

Additionally, when you die, any remaining balance in your annuity can go to your named beneficiary without making a huge dent in your withdrawal payment amount, as it does with lifetime annuities. You may incur a surrender penalty if you withdraw more than the 10% free withdrawal during the 10-year penalty period, but at least your principal is intact and you have access to it if needed. Surrender charges in most fixed indexed annuities usually last for 10 years but are waived immediately upon the death of the owner or when taking lifetime payments or 10% annual free withdrawals.

Finally, the fees for a fixed indexed annuity are almost always lower than with variable annuities. Instead of paying close to 4% for greater risk, most fixed indexed annuities charge around 1% for the strategies described in previous chapters—and some of them don't have a rider charge at all!

12 The withdrawal will reduce your income proportionate to the amount taken.

So, to review, a fixed indexed annuity offers you strategies that maximize your principal and insulate you from market risk. They're also less expensive and more flexible than any other annuity product. It's not surprising that ERISA has now recommended including annuities into corporate sponsored plans.

Finding You the Best Fixed Indexed Lifeboat

Here's the challenge with this lifeboat. Unlike Social Security, it isn't guaranteed by law; you're going to have to make this switch yourself. The government isn't going to change over your IRA for you. And, unlike Social Security, a fixed indexed annuity isn't free. Every retirement account costs something, even when they're extremely consumer friendly. In fact, there can be a lot of variability in terms of costs and benefits, even with the fixed indexed annuity.

I don't favor people paying 4% on their annuity when they don't have to. That's just too high a cost to pay when you are trying to get your retirement income to take you as far as you need to go.

That's why I've put together a list of the top 18 companies that offer fixed indexed annuities in this country. The cost for their lifeboats all fall between 0 and 1.5% per year.

If you would like a copy of this list, simply go to my website, www.accessretirementgroup.com, and fill out a short form on the Annuities page. That way, you can begin the process of placing your money in a retirement account that makes sense for your needs, without market risk and at a price that is fair.

Running for the Last Lifeboat When the Ship Is Going Down

Whether you've done everything right financially in your life or made some mistakes, there are times when you may discover you're going to need a bigger lifeboat.

Perhaps Social Security is less than you expected. Perhaps you took that lump-sum retirement offer or stayed put and saw your income drop lower than expected. Or maybe retirement was just more expensive than you planned.

Thankfully, we've still got one lifeboat left on deck. So, if the ship is already going down, and there are no other seaworthy vessels left, it's time to run to the last and safest option for you: the unsinkable lifeboat.

Part IV

The Unsinkable Lifeboat

Chapter 12.

When the Ship's Going Down and the Surf Is Rough

Even after maximizing Social Security and maximizing retirement account income through a fixed indexed annuity, some people still find that they're short of their needs. There's just too much month at the end of their money.

This is always the worst-case scenario for people. At that point, most people are past the age when they can realistically supplement by going back to work. There's just a gap between their needs and their income, and if they don't do something, they're going to fall into it.

Now, the ship they are on is going down, and all the standard lifeboats are underwater. That's a desperate feeling, and I want to do my best to make sure you never have to experience it.

That's why we're going to cover one last lifeboat in this book. And luckily for you, no matter the waves, this lifeboat is unsinkable.

The Do-It-Yourself Tax-Free Pension

For those of you who find yourself—or worry you will find yourself—in the previously described predicament, I like to call this final lifeboat the "Do-It-Yourself Tax-Free Pension." This is a program tailor-made for people who are struggling to find the resources to get through retirement comfortably. I mean, it was literally made with that person in mind. The program that allows for the Do-It-Yourself Tax-Free Pension was created back in 1989 by the federal government as a supplement to the Old-Age, Survivors, and Disability Act of 1935, which gave us Social Security. The government saw that people were living longer and that Social Security couldn't keep up. Because incomes had been flat over the last decade, many didn't have enough savings to cover for a Social Security shortfall.

In other words, far too many people were falling into that gap, and the government couldn't afford to cover the difference.

Another issue was the cost of long-term care. The government was paying $28 billion for long-term care through Medi-Cal and Medicaid. Looking at all those factors—increased longevity, stalled incomes that led to smaller savings, and increased long-term care costs—the government projected that their budget for long-term care coverage for people who were impoverished would double over the next 20 years if they didn't come up with another way to help people with their retirement financial needs.

This program was their solution to that problem. And it worked so well, it's still their solution to your problem today.

The Other Name for the Do-It-Yourself Tax-Free Pension

At this point, I have to come clean with you. You've probably heard of this program, but not by the name I've given it up to this point. What you've heard it called is a reverse mortgage.

Before you kick this book across the floor and call me a charlatan, let me tell you that the reason I introduced this program by a different name is because I want you to look at it with fresh eyes. Just like with the fixed indexed annuity, you may have been prejudiced against this option for no good reason. Many people get bad information about reverse mortgages, and that leads them to dismiss this option even when they need it. I know, because I was one of those people.

So forget everything you've heard about the reverse mortgage. All I want you to do is give me a few pages to explain why everything you thought you knew about this program may be wrong, and why this program could save your retirement.

Dad's Reverse Mortgage

For many years, I was NOT fond of reverse mortgages. I mean, I really didn't like them. In fact, I used to commit whole seminars to talking people out of them. I felt this was a dangerous program, and at that time, I wouldn't have dreamed of recommending it to a client or even an enemy.

But then, my first client changed my mind again. In 2005, I got a call from my dad. The call went something like this:

"Hi Mark, this is Dad."

"I know your voice, Dad. How are you doing? How can I help?"

There was the shortest of pauses, and then clearing his throat, Dad said, "Mark, your mom and I are considering doing a reverse mortgage."

When I heard him say that, I jumped out of my chair. "Over my dead retirement-planning body you are. You're not going to do one of those! Not on my watch!"

My dad gave me a moment to collect myself, and he walked me back through his and Mom's financial situation. "Mark, you remember that I took my Social Security benefits at 62, right? Well, that cost Mom and I a permanent 25% reduction in benefits."

"Yeah," I said, still somewhat smarting from this fact more than a decade later. "I remember."

"And you remember that I serviced pools in Beverly Hills for 40 years, and I never made tons of money. So, while you helped me make the most of my retirement savings through those fixed indexed annuities, my monthly income is still not enough to allow me to retire comfortably."

"I know that, Dad."

"Well, Southern California is quite an expensive place to live, Mark, especially when you receive 25% less from Social Security and only have a modest income from other retirement accounts."

I still wasn't convinced. I told him again, though less forcefully, "Not on my watch."

And he told me, "Mark, this isn't your watch. It's mine. But if you want to talk this out, there's an FHA lender coming to the house today at 5 o'clock."

As soon as we were off the phone, I got to work rallying the troops. I called my wife, Cathy, I called my kids, and most importantly, I called my three sisters.

"Girls," I told them, "Mom and Dad need our help. They're about to sign the house away with a reverse mortgage. We've got to go over there and talk them out of it."

So, we all put on our best clothing. I put on my best dark suit and a red tie, the outfit that made me look particularly intimidatingly professional and knowledgeable. We descended upon Mom and Dad's home in Dana Point for the purpose of confronting this dirty rat FHA lender who had the audacity to try to cheat my parents into a reverse mortgage.

These days, I feel bad for that FHA lender. He turned out to be a nice, soft-spoken man, and he was not prepared for a whole family on the warpath, all heading right for him. Luckily for him, though, before I could rip the guy to shreds, Dad stepped in between us.

Now, my dad is a very pleasant guy. His nickname is Mild-Mannered Mel. So you can imagine the surprise to all of us when my mild-mannered dad stepped into the middle of the battlefield and told me to sit down.

I started to protest, but Dad wouldn't have it.

"Before any of you open your mouth, I'd like to say something."

The room grew quiet. "Mark, your mind is like a parachute. It only works when it's open."

He stunned me with that statement. And the following statement stunned me even more.

"A closed mind, like a closed parachute, is worthless!"

He continued, "What I'd like you, your family, and your sisters to do is to close your mouth for a moment and open your ears, and perhaps you might learn something about this program. Now, I know you know a lot, and I know you think you know everything about reverse mortgages. But maybe—just maybe—there's still something you can learn."

Duly chastened, I sat there in silence and let the meek FHA lender give his presentation.

About midway through, my dad interrupted. He clearly felt that he had been a little hard on me, so he decided to ask me a few softball questions to build me back up and reengage me.

"My son here is a successful retirement advisor," he told the FHA lender. "If you don't mind, I'd like to ask him to help out with the presentation."

The FHA lender gave Dad and me the floor. Dad continued, "Mark, why don't you explain to the group what a pension is."

I sat up, straightened my red tie, and said, "That's a great question, Dad. A pension is something that you put money into, usually on a monthly basis, for purposes of retirement."

My dad interrupted, "Kind of like a mortgage payment, right?"

"Well, sort of. As you put money into this account, your equity begins to grow."

My dad said, "Kind of like the equity in my home."

"Well, sort of. As this equity grows, you have this large amount of money that you can access for retirement income."

My dad interrupted for a third time. "Mark, do you remember what I paid for this home?"

"Of course. You paid $39,500."

"Do you know what it's worth today?"

"I'd guess around $800,000."

"Mark, you have been our retirement advisor for years and you know what our income and expenses are. So, you know as well as anybody that we are the proverbial house rich and cash challenged. We have all of this equity built up in our home, and we need that equity to help us through our golden years."

I couldn't argue with that, so I sat there silently. Then, Dad said, "I know you've helped thousands of clients retire comfortably over the years. Have you ever had a client who had a tax-free pension, really needed the money from that pension, but decided to give it away to someone else?"

"No one would do that. In fact, advising someone to do that would be akin to elder abuse."

"But Mark," my dad said, "that's exactly what you're asking me to do. This is our equity. We bought this home. We put those monthly contributions in. We worked and waited and watched as our equity grew in this property. This is *our* pension. And I have to plan for *our* retirement, not *yours*."

The Faucet on the Edge of My Property

Dad could see he was finally winning me over. So he took advantage of my new openness and explained the reverse mortgage in terms I'd never considered before.

"What the government is allowing us to do is to put a faucet on the edge of our property, where we can access up to between 50% and 60% of our hard-earned equity. Remember, that's our equity, not your equity. They're going to let us pull out these payments tax-free. With a regular pension, any withdrawals would be taxed as ordinary income. But with this program, we'll get to receive a portion of our much-deserved capital gains and receive them on a tax-free basis through this FHA-insured loan program. With the money coming through that tax-free faucet, combined with my Social Security and annuity income, your mother and I can live comfortably for the rest of our days.

"Now," he continued, "let's say your mother and I live on for years and years to come, and we drain off $400,000 of our equity through that faucet. We'd still be able to leave you and your sisters the remainder of the equity in this house. If you only sell the house for what it's worth today, you and your sisters would still inherit approximately $400,000. And you'll get that money tax-free as well. So, Mark, considering our situation and those numbers, does this sound like a good plan or not?"

I had to admit it. I told him, "That doesn't sound like a good plan. It sounds like an amazing plan."

In that very moment, I realized that I had completely miscalculated this program and the nice FHA lender who had explained it to my parents. I had thought a reverse mortgage meant you just gave your home away to the federal government. In fact, the program ensures that's not even possible in most circumstances. Instead, when you use this program right, there's usually plenty of equity left over for your heirs. I had also been taught that if someone's parents died owing more than the value of the house on their loans, the children would have to cover the difference. Again, I had it backward. The reverse mortgage is designed to make sure that is *never* the case. All reverse mortgages come with gap insurance protection—which we'll discuss in more detail in the next chapter—to cover the heirs if the loan balance exceeds the value of the home upon the borrower's passing.

Every negative thing I'd heard about this program was wrong. In fact, it was designed to make sure those nightmares could never happen. Thanks to Dad, and that wonderful FHA lender, I finally understood just what a powerful tool the reverse mortgage could be. And I have been a proponent ever since!

Chapter 13.

The Pension of the Baby Boomer Generation

The reverse mortgage used to be seen as a rare, last-ditch, break-in-case-of-fire financial option. Not anymore. It's become one of the most important retirement tools for an entire generation. According to the National Reverse Mortgage Lenders Association, back in 2000, only 2,000 retirees took advantage of this program over the whole year. By 2004, approximately 7,000 retirees *per month* were applying for this life-altering loan program. That rise coincides with the Baby Boomer generation beginning to hit retirement. In essence, this has become the pension for the Baby Boomer generation.

The people getting reverse mortgages these days come from every kind of background, but they all have two things in common: They own their homes, and their other lifeboats weren't going to carry them the whole way through retirement.

For many of us, our home is the biggest investment we ever make. It can be worth far more than our entire retirement account, particularly if your home is in California. Using the equity in your home can be a powerful financial tool that can increase your quality of life during a long—or health-impaired—retirement.

Now that you know the truth about reverse mortgages, it's time to find out how to use it.

What Is a Reverse Mortgage *Really*?

We've talked around the reverse mortgage a great deal so far. But when you get down to it, what is a reverse mortgage *really*?

The technical name for a reverse mortgage is a Home Equity Conversion Mortgage, or HECM. It is similar to a regular conventional loan in which you maintain the title to your home, pay the property taxes and the homeowners insurance, accrue interest and pay closing costs, keep your home up and do scheduled maintenance, have the option to sell or refinance your home at any time, and leave your home to your heirs upon passing.

However, there are some key differences. First, you have to be 62 or older in order to obtain a reverse mortgage. You must also live in your home and maintain it as your primary residence. Additionally, the loan is due and payable when you die, sell the home, or leave the home permanently to enter an adult care facility.

With a conventional loan, you have one payment option—you make the mortgage payment or the lender takes your home. With a reverse mortgage, you have several payment options. You can:

- Make an interest-only payment
- Pay down the principal

- Elect to make no payment at all (this is the most popular option) without the risk of foreclosure and losing your home

With any of those payment options, the government won't come and take your house because mortgage payments are NOT required with a reverse mortgage, they're optional!

You can also receive money from a reverse mortgage loan in several different ways. You can:

- Elect to receive a lump sum to pay off debts or make necessary home repairs or improvements
- Receive a tax-free, lifetime monthly income to supplement Social Security and pension income
- Open a line of credit that increases every time you celebrate a birthday and save the money for a rainy day
- Receive a monthly income, a lump sum, and/or a line of credit simultaneously

The architects of this loan program purposely built in a lot of flexibility, so you can use it to meet your individual financial and retirement needs.

The Cost of a Reverse Mortgage

The reverse mortgage is a fantastic financial option, but it doesn't come to you free of charge. There are costs, and you should know them up front.

Those costs start with gap insurance, which is a policy designed to cover the difference if you take out more from a reverse mortgage than your home can eventually be sold for. It protects your inheritors so they never have to worry about owing more than the value of the home. It is required and included as part of the costs of your reverse mortgage. And it usually comes to 2% of the value of the property. So if your home is worth $700,000, you must pay a lump sum of $14,000 in gap insurance as part of your financed closing costs before you can obtain your reverse mortgage. There is also an ongoing mortgage insurance premium equal to .5% of the loan balance charged for the life of the loan.

In addition, there are other up-front financed closing costs of approximately $2,700 for escrow and title insurance, plus an origination fee of up to $6,000 that may be charged by some lenders. All of these up-front closing costs are wrapped into the reverse mortgage loan balance and no out-of-pocket expenses are required. The only out-of-pocket costs required are the following:

- All reverse mortgage borrowers are required to pay approximately $150 for a third-party HUD counseling interview to determine suitability and borrower readiness to proceed with the loan.
- An appraisal fee of approximately $475 must be paid by the borrower to determine home value and property condition before the loan is approved. Some lenders allow the appraisal fee to be added to the loan balance.

So if you were looking to receive a $100,000 lump sum from your reverse mortgage, your initial loan balance would be approximately $122,700 to cover all the costs. Additionally, the interest on the loan—about 5%—will accrue on the $122,700 balance, even though you only received an advance of $100,000.

Now, the interest payments will be deferred and added on to the total cost of the loan after you pass. That interest will be taken out of the sale of your home, which will decrease how much your heirs inherit. So there's an up-front cost and an ongoing cost to pay for a reverse mortgage.

The ABCs of Deciding on a Reverse Mortgage

The previously mentioned costs come to quite a lot of money, and that money is usually the chief complaint I hear about the reverse mortgage.

However, every option has a cost. My recommendation has always been that before pursuing a reverse mortgage, it is wise to consider the cost of your other options in gaining access to the equity in your home before going forward. I have come to refer to this cost analysis as the A B C D Es of Reverse Mortgage Costs Alternatives. Here's how it works—assuming an available lump sum of $350,000 at closing and a home value of $700,000:

A – Option A stands for doing **A**bsolutely nothing with your home's equity. What is the cost of this option you might ask? On the surface, you could say it costs nothing, but upon further examination, the real cost is far more. By doing nothing, you pay a huge opportunity cost because you never receive the $350,000 locked up in your home's equity. All the things you could have done with that money are off the table. This is the equivalent of giving *your* $350,000 tax-free pension to someone else. If giving your pension away sounds absurd, then you can consider Option B.

B – Option B stands for **B**orrowing using conventional methods by getting a Home Equity Line of Credit (HELOC) from the bank. These are relatively inexpensive to set up. The closing costs on a HELOC are nowhere near the $22,700 required for a reverse mortgage. But up-front costs aside, is Option B really that good of a deal? The real cost of Option B is ongoing mortgage payments of $1,670.95 per month—the current cost for a $350,000 mortgage—for the rest of your life. Most retirees I meet are trying to *reduce* their monthly expenses, not increase them. Many retirees fall into the trap of borrowing from a HELOC and then having to borrow *more* just to make their payments. Some literally borrow themselves out of their homes. If the prospect of getting swallowed up in the quicksand of debt during your golden years does not sound appealing, then consider Option C.

C – Option C stands for **C**hildren. If you really think you need an extra $350,000 to sustain you throughout your retirement, then Option C suggests that you call your children and get the money from them. That seems fair. You have always been there for them, and now, it's their turn to be there for you. Maybe in principle, but that's not how most retirees—or their children—feel about it in practice. Most retired clients I speak with would rather fall on a sword than burden their children with their retirement shortcomings—assuming they even have children. If that is true for you, you need to consider Option D.

D – Option D stands for **D**ispose of the property. If you really need the money captured in the walls and mortar of your home, Option D suggests you just sell your home. What are the costs of selling your home? For starters, if your home is valued at $700,000, the closing costs on a home of that value—including real estate commissions—is approximately $45,500. Then, you have to pay the movers $5,000-$10,000 to move you to your new home. If you can't afford to buy a new home, you can put your $644,500 in the bank at 1% and get $6,445 per year in before-tax income and receive around $537 per month to pay your new landlord. If a bill of $55,500 and monthly rent—plus the inconveniences of potentially moving to a new area—does not appeal to you, then you still have Option E to consider.

E – Option E stands for **E**xecute a reverse mortgage. With a financed closing cost of *only* $22,700, you can remain in your home forever without a mortgage payment, gain access to your $350,000 tax-free pension, and receive your money in any form you need it. Back in my neighborhood, we used to call this option "Having Your Cake and Eating It, Too."

As you can see, after doing the math and considering all the costs behind each of your options, the reverse mortgage often turns out to be the most cost-effective choice.

Who Needs a Reverse Mortgage?

I'm sure all of this sounds pretty great up to this point, but before you jump into this lifeboat, we need to make sure you need to get in. The reverse mortgage is very useful in many circumstances, but it isn't for everyone.

As with any financial product, there are costs and drawbacks to the reverse mortgage. As we'll see shortly, there is a very strenuous process you have to go through to make sure you are the right candidate for this lifeboat.

Before you launch this boat, it's worth considering whether either of the four main reasons to get a reverse mortgage apply to you.

Reason #1: Pay Off Your Mortgage

The most common motivation for reverse mortgage purchasers is to pay off an existing mortgage.

Let's say you're 70 years old, you have a $3,000-a-month mortgage payment, and only $2,500 coming in from Social Security. In that scenario, you have to live on whatever your retirement accounts provide you minus the $500 you need to cover the difference between your Social Security and your mortgage. That's a very difficult situation. With a reverse mortgage, you can pay off your current mortgage entirely and replace it with a zero-payment loan, freeing up your entire Social Security and retirement account income.

Imagine the difference that would make to your quality of life. And, potentially, your reverse mortgage may still have money left over that can pay for other expenses, loans or bills.

Reason #2: Getting Out From Under a Too-Big Mortgage

This is very similar to reason #1, but it is different in a crucial way. Let's say that 70-year-old from the previous example has a similar mortgage payment, but the remaining balance on the mortgage is $450,000, and the reverse mortgage can only provide $350,000 in lump-sum relief. What are they to do then?

This scenario comes up from time to time. And, when it's appropriate and a viable option, I advise clients to do the following: Take the lump sum from the reverse mortgage for $350,000 and combine it with $100,000 from savings. With these two resources combined, you can pay off your current mortgage and live off your other sources of income debt-free.

With the elimination of a $3,000 monthly mortgage payment, that amounts to $36,000 in cash flow savings per year. Just ask yourself what retirement plan is going to offer you a $36,000 annual return on an investment of $100,000? That's a 36% return on investment for life!

Reason #3: Cover Long-Term Care

Sometimes, the decision to take out a reverse mortgage has nothing to do with the person's home. Instead, the homeowner, their spouse, or another loved one requires long-term care, and their current financial resources can't cover those needs.

Unless you already have long-term care insurance, a reverse mortgage can offer you a good way to free up funds for that needed healthcare coverage. Remember, the interest on this loan is very modest, and you will never have to repay it, unless you sell or permanently leave the home. When it comes to healthcare, it's rare you find a *cost-efficient* solution, but that's just what a reverse mortgage can be!

Reason #4: Live Your Retirement Well

Finally, there are some people who don't have mortgage or health concerns. They're in a decent financial position, and they don't *need* a reverse mortgage in the way others do.

However, they may still *want* one. I've had plenty of clients come to me and say, "I've paid off my house, and I have $1 million in equity just sitting dormant. The kids are all doing well. They don't need the money. And I can't take this house with me when I die. So I want to enjoy my retirement and live before it's too late!"

These individuals are looking to enjoy the years they have ahead, and I think they're right to do so. I always tell my clients that if they want to travel, try new experiences, or just relax in the kind of comfort they always denied themselves, the early years of retirement are the time to do it. Between 60 and about 75, most of us will enjoy good health. Beyond that, good health is less guaranteed. That money you could have enjoyed can easily end up paying for healthcare later.

So if you want a boat or you want to spend a year traveling around South America, the reverse mortgage is a way you can do that.

Muriel's Reverse Mortgage

The reverse mortgage can offer you an amazing amount of financial flexibility. Sometimes, it can even increase the amount you leave to your family after your passing. That's even possible after you take out the money you need from it.

That's just what happened with Muriel, one of my former clients. She did a reverse mortgage on her home in 2006, not because she needed the income but because she needed access to a line of credit on her home. The government offered her a $328,000 line of credit, and she promptly took out $75,000 to cover her major expenses.

And that was it, or so it seemed. We lost touch after the process was completed, and I didn't hear from her again until 2010, when Muriel called me out of the blue.

"Mark," she said, "I have a question for you, and I really need an answer."

"Okay, Muriel. Nice to hear from you again. How can I help?"

She jumped right into her concerns. "What happens when I die with this reverse mortgage?"

"Well," I said, "What happens is, your children would receive the home, and then, they would have up to one year in which to sell it and pay off the debt you incurred through your reverse mortgage. The difference between the sale and the debt would become their inheritance."

There was a long pause, during which I could tell I hadn't made Muriel feel any better. So I decided to dig into her particular circumstances.

"Let's work through the specifics of your loan," I said. "How much did you borrow from your reverse mortgage?"

"Just the $75,000 we took out initially."

"Okay, great," I said, "And what's the home worth today?"

"That's the problem," Muriel told me. "When we took out the loan back in 2006, the home was worth about $490,000. Today, after the bubble burst, my home's valued at only $175,000."

Her home was in Palm Springs, an area that was crushed by the real estate crisis in 2008-09.

"I'm sorry to hear that, Muriel. In that case, your children could sell the house for $175,000, pay back the $75,000—plus a little interest—and receive about $100,000 in inheritance."

"That seems fair," she said slowly, but something was still on her mind. I waited while she formulated her next question.

"But, Mark, what do I do with this remaining line of credit I've got?"

"Well, how much is in the line of credit?"

She checked her most recent statement. "The line of credit has grown to a value of $300,000."

"You've got to be kidding me! Let me review this. Your home is worth $175,000 today, but your available line of credit is $300,000?"

"Yes," she said. The line of credit had grown independent of the value of her property. The loan was based on how much her home had been worth *at the time* of the reverse mortgage origination. So that line of credit continued to gain value over the years she didn't take out money. At that point, her line of credit far exceeded the total value of her home.

"Muriel, I want you to listen very carefully. Take a $300,000 advance from your line of credit and deposit the money in the bank. When and if you do this, your reverse mortgage loan balance will increase to approximately $375,000. Then, when you eventually pass away, your children will have to sell your house and repay the full value of the loan with the proceeds from the sale of your home—approximately $175,000. The debt from the loan will be greater than the value of your home, but the shortfall will be covered by that gap insurance policy that you paid for up front and have been paying for on a monthly basis. Your children won't get a cent from the sale of your house, but they'll have $300,000 waiting for them to inherit at the bank. That's $200,000 more than they would receive if you do nothing. And that's still $125,000 more than they would have gotten if they had sold the house without you taking this reverse mortgage. Because you have this resource, you'll provide them with so much more!"

Muriel became so excited, she actually dropped the phone. But she followed my advice, and she set aside a large inheritance for her children, even though the value of her home had plummeted when the economy hit an iceberg.

How to Get a Reverse Mortgage

Okay, at this point, you can see there's a lot of upside to getting a reverse mortgage, but how do you actually get one?

One of the best advertisements for the reverse mortgage is just how rigorous the application process is. To begin with, a reverse mortgage can't be sold, not in the way you think about other financial products. It isn't as simple as an FHA lender showing up, offering you a reverse mortgage, getting you to sign on the dotted line, and handing you a check. Instead, a reverse mortgage can only be explained. Then, if the homeowner is interested, a complex, multistep process begins.

In order for a homeowner to qualify, not only do they need to consult with an FHA lender, they also have to go to a third-party called HUD counseling. That third-party counselor consults with the borrower in an hour-long phone conversation to confirm that the homeowner knows about the costs, as well as how the reverse mortgage can address their wants and needs. It's this third-party counselor, not the lender, who decides whether or not the homeowner can actually benefit from this program and whether they understand the program and their alternatives.

Once they pass the scrutiny of this HUD-appointed counselor can they be approved for the program. And only at that point can the FHA lender start the actual loan process.

This system is designed to protect the homeowner above all else by ensuring only those who can really benefit and who fully understand the process can receive the loan. You can't be tricked into a reverse mortgage, and even after you receive one, there are laws in place to make sure your FHA lender can't push you to invest in certain areas that would particularly benefit that lender. It's as scam-free a process as you can imagine.

There are further restrictions still. In April 2015, the federal government began requiring homeowners to pass a financial assessment before they could qualify for a reverse mortgage. Now, you have to have relatively good credit, and you have to prove that you can pay your property taxes and your insurance. If you can't prove those things, the lender is required to set aside certain funds from your reverse mortgage proceeds to pay for those expenses. This is designed to limit the access of frivolous borrowers to the program.

Keep in mind, these are just the basics of the reverse mortgage. It's clearly a complex process and complex program, and I would always recommend you contact an expert advisor before proceeding any further. If you would like, ACCESS Reverse Lending Group is prepared to provide the numbers, the details, and an illustration of how the process works. We can also determine whether you qualify for the program and whether it would be useful in your circumstances.

Time to Get in the Lifeboat

Throughout this book, we've discovered that what may have once seemed like no more than driftwood has turned out to be a series of lifeboats that can save almost any retirement, even when we hit a massive iceberg in our economy.

If any of these lifeboats seem attractive to you, I am ready to help you work through the complicated details and to advise you on the best lifeboat options to get you off this ship and into clear, warm waters for the entirety of your retirement.

Conclusion

I hope this book has been of use to you and your family. Having watched my own parents struggle with retirement, my aim here has been to make it easier for you to gain access to the lifeboats you need, particularly with the economic risks ahead.

I'm sure if any of us could go back to the day before the launch of the Titanic, we'd all do what we could to avoid that tragedy, and that's exactly what I'm trying to do here.

I hope that everyone who reads this is able to say to their loved ones the same thing my dad said to me a short while ago when I went over to see him and asked how he's doing.

"Well, Mark," he said, "I'm 88, and I'm hitting the gym three times a week, so I can't complain."

"No, Dad, I mean financially. How are you doing?"

He looked me straight in the eyes, and he said, "Honestly, Mark, these days, I have more than enough."

If you follow the advice in this book and work with an experienced financial advisor, you too can have "more than enough" to sail through your retirement, however long it lasts.

I Believe in These Products

The lifeboats we've covered in this book aren't hypothetical to me, they're lifeboats I've settled my own family in. I'm a consumer of these products, just like my father. I've organized my Social Security around the principles in this book. I own annuities, and when I retire, I will have the capacity to generate multiple income streams that can never be outlived. And I know, if the day arrives when the ship starts going down and I need an unsinkable lifeboat, the first place I'll look will be a reverse mortgage.

I tell you this because I want you to know that I believe in what I'm sharing here. I live by my own advice. When I get up in front of an audience and explain these ideas, I'm not just some insurance guy talking about something that I've heard about. I'm not just some lender looking to make a buck. I've lived the experience of having these products. I've seen what happens when someone makes the wrong choices with their lifeboats.

My parents were my first clients, and they taught me that everyone who comes into my office is somebody's parent or somebody's loved one. And they deserve to be taken care of just like Mom and Dad. Family is important to me, and I try to advise every client the same way I'd advise anyone in my family.

Contact Us to Learn More

We have 37 seconds until this economy hits an iceberg, and I consider it my duty to get as many of you into lifeboats as possible. There won't be any partially filled, misused lifeboats on my watch. I'm an expert in these matters, so whatever lifeboat is going to take you to financial safety, that's the one we're going to use.

When you're ready to talk about your retirement plans—whether it's just maximizing Social Security, reinvesting that 401(k) in a more stable and secure annuity, or, as a last resort, pursuing a reverse mortgage—I'm ready to help.

You can contact me at ACCESS Retirement Advisory Group any time at 949-422-6907 or email me at mark@accessretirementgroup.com. If it's more convenient, I'm happy to come meet you where you are.

You can also go to www.accessretirementgroup.com to fill out a form to receive your free 22-page Social Security Maximization booklet and a list of the Top Fixed Indexed Annuity Providers in the country.

Thank you for reading this book. I look forward to helping you set sail to a safe and comfortable retirement.

About the Author

Mark Andra is the founder of ACCESS Retirement Advisory Group.

After graduating from the Marriott School of Management with a degree in Business/Marketing, Mark immediately entered the workforce at First Union Investment Corporation in San Francisco as an income property broker.

Mark's experience in real estate and mortgage lending uniquely qualifies him to speak to real estate owners and real estate professionals about their retirement needs and challenges. Coupled with his 30 years of experience in insurance and retirement planning, Mark has the special ability to craft innovative and creative solutions that protect and grow your retirement assets.

Mark receives his greatest joy from his family. Mark has been married to his college sweetheart, Cathy, for 38 years and is the proud father of four married children and nine grandchildren—with two more on the way! Mark is an avid reader, recreational golfer, and a lifelong fitness and health enthusiast.

Professional Licenses

California Life and Disability License
California Real Estate Broker and NMLS Licensed
NSSA — National Social Security Advisor

Made in the USA
Monee, IL
04 November 2026

67387218R00075